Rambles in the Mammoth Cave, during the Year 1844

Alexander Clark Bullitt

Contents

PUBLISHER'S ADVERTISEMENT..7
INTERESTING FACTS. 10
TABLE OF DISTANCES. 11
CHAPTER I. 14
CHAPTER II. 21
CHAPTER III. 28
CHAPTER IV. 31
CHAPTER V. 35
CHAPTER VI. 40
CHAPTER VII. 44
CHAPTER VIII. 48
CHAPTER IX. 51
CHAPTER X. 56

RAMBLES IN THE MAMMOTH CAVE, DURING THE YEAR 1844

BY
Alexander Clark Bullitt

PUBLISHER'S ADVERTISEMENT.

To meet the calls so frequently made upon as by intelligent visitors to our City, for some work descriptive of the Mammoth Cave, we are, at length, enabled to present the public a succinct, but instructive narrative of a visit to this "Wonder of Wonders," from the pen of a gentleman, who, without professing to have explored ALL that is curious or beautiful or sublime in its vast recesses, has yet seen every thing that has been seen by others, and has described enough to quicken and enlighten the curiosity of those who have never visited it.

Aware of the embarrassment which most persons experience who design visiting the Cave, owing to the absence of any printed itinerary of the various routes leading to it, we have supplied, in the present volume, this desideratum, from information received from reliable persons residing on the different roads here enumerated. The road from Louisville to the Cave, and thence to Nashville, is graded the entire distance, and the greater part of it M'Adamized. From Louisville to the mouth of Salt river, twenty miles, the country is level, with a rich alluvial soil, probably at some former period the bed of a lake. A few miles below the former place and extending to the latter, a chain of elevated hills is seen to the South-East, affording beautiful and picturesque situations for country seats, and strangely overlooked by the rich and tasteful. The river is crossed by a ferry, and the traveler is put down at a comfortable inn in the village of West Point. Two miles from the mouth of Salt river, begins the ascent of Muldrow's Hill. The road is excellent, and having elevated hills on either side, is highly romantic to its summit, five miles. From the top of this hill to Elizabethtown, the country is well settled, though the improvements are generally indifferent--the soil thin, but well adapted to small-grain, and oak the prevailing growth. Elizabethtown, twenty-five miles from the mouth of Salt river, is quite a pretty and flourishing village, built chiefly of brick, with several churches and three large inns. From this place to Nolin creek, the distance is ten miles. Here there is a small town, containing some ten or twelve log houses, a large saw and grist mill, and a comfortable and very neat inn, kept by Mr. Mosher. Immediately after crossing this creek, the traveler enters "Yankee Street," as the inhabitants style this section of the road. For a distance of ten or twelve miles from Nolin toward Bacon creek, the land belongs, or did belong to the former Postmaster General, Gideon Granger, and on either side of the road, to the extent of Mr. G.'s possessions, are settlements made by emigrants from New York and the New England States. From Bacon creek to Munfordsville, eight miles, the country is pleasantly undulating, and here, indeed the whole route from Elizabethtown to the Cave, passes through what was until recently a Prairie, or, in the language of the country, "Barrens," and renders it highly interesting, especially to the botanist, from the multitude and variety of flowers with which it abounds during the Spring and Autumn months. Munfordsville, and Woodsonville directly opposite, are situated on Green river, on high and broken ground. They are small places, in each of which, however, are comfortable inns. Boats laden with tobacco and other produce, descend from this point and from a considerable distance above, to New Orleans. About two and a half miles beyond Munfordsville, the new State road to the Cave, (virtually made by Dr. Croghan, at a great expense,) leaves the Turnpike, and joins it again at the Dripping Springs, eight miles below, on the route to Nashville. This road, in going from Louisville to Nashville, is not only the shortest by three and a half miles, but to the Cave it is from ten to twelve miles shorter than the one taken by visiters previous to its construction. It therefore lessens the inconvenience, delay and consequent expense to which travelers were formerly subjected. The road itself is an excellent one, the country through which it passes highly picturesque, and Dr. Croghan has entitled himself to the gratitude of the traveling community by his liberality and enterprise in constructing it.

Persons visiting the Cave by Steamer, (a boat leaves Louisville for Bowling-Green every week) will find much to interest them in the admirable locks and dams, rendering the navigation of Green river safe and good at all seasons for boats of a large class. Passengers can obtain conveyances at all times and at moderate rates, from Bowling-Green, by the Dripping Spring, to the Cave, distant twenty-two miles. Fifteen miles of this road is M'Adamized, the remainder is graded and not inferior to the finished portion. The last eight miles from the Dripping Spring to the Cave, cannot fail to excite the admiration of every one who delights in beholding wild and beautiful scenery. A visit to the Cedar Springs on this route, is alone worth a journey of many miles. Passengers on the upper turnpike, from Bardstown to Nashville, can, on reaching Glasgow, at all times procure conveyances to the Cave, either by Bell's or by Prewett's Knob.

Arrived at the Cave, the visitor alights at a spacious hotel, the general arrangements, attendance and *cuisine* of which, are adapted to the most fastidious taste. He feels that as far as the "creature comforts" are necessary to enjoyment, the prospect is full of promise; nor will he be disappointed. And now, this first and most important preliminary to a traveler settled to his perfect content, he may remain for weeks and experience daily gratification, "**Stephen** his guide," in wandering through some of its two hundred and twenty-six avenues--in gazing, until he is oppressed with the feeling of their magnificence, at some of its forty-seven domes,--in listening, until their drowsy murmurs pain the sense, to some of its many waterfalls,--or haply intent upon discovery, he hails some new vista, or fretted roof, or secret river, or unsounded lake, or crystal fountain, with as much rapture as Balboa, from "that peak in Darien," gazed on the Pacific; he is assured that he "has a poet," and an historian too. Stephen has linked his name to dome, or avenue, or river, and it is already immortal--in the Cave.

Independent of the attractions to be found in the Cave, there is much above ground to gratify the different tastes of visiters. There is a capacious ball-room, ninety feet by thirty, with a fine band of music,--a ten-pin alley,--romantic walks and carriage-drives in all directions, rendered easy of access by the fine road recently finished. The many rare and beautiful flowers in the immediate vicinity of the Cave, invite to exercise, and bouquets as exquisite as were ever culled in garden or green-house, may be obtained even as late as August. The fine sport the neighborhood affords to the hunter and the angler--Green river, just at hand, offers such "store of fish," as father Walton or his son and disciple Cotton, were they alive again, would love to meditate and angle in!--and the woods! Capt. Scott or Christopher North himself, might grow weary of the sight of game, winged or quadruped.

INTERESTING FACTS.

1. Accidents of no kind have ever occurred in the Mammoth Cave.
2. Visiters, going in or coming out of the Cave, are not liable to contract colds; on the contrary, colds are commonly relieved by a visit in the Cave.
3. No impure air exists in any part of the Cave.
4. Reptiles, of no description, have ever been seen in the Cave; on the contrary, they, as well as quadrupeds, avoid it.
5. Combustion is perfect in all parts of the Cave.
6. Decomposition and consequent putrefaction are unobservable in all parts of the Cave.
7. The water of the Cave is of the purest kind; and, besides fresh water, there are one or two sulphur springs.
8. There are two hundred and twenty-six Avenues in the Cave; forty-seven Domes; eight Cataracts, and twenty-three Pits.
9. The temperature of the Cave is 59 deg. Fahrenheit, and remains so, uniformly, winter and Summer.
10. No sound, not even the loudest peal of thunder, is heard one quarter of a mile in the Cave.

* * * * *

The author of "Rambles in the Mammoth Cave," has written a scientific account of the Cave, embracing its Geology, Mineralogy, etc., which we could not, in time, insert in this publication.

TABLE OF DISTANCES.

FROM LOUISVILLE TO MAMMOTH CAVE.

Medley's	10 miles.
Mouth Salt River	10
Trueman's	8
Haycraft's	7
Elizabethtown	9
Nolin	9
Lucas	11
Munfordsville	10
Mammoth Cave	14-1/2

	88-1/2 miles.

FROM LEXINGTON TO MAMMOTH CAVE.

Harrodsburgh	20 miles.
Perryville	10
Frosts	12
Young	4
Lebanon	7
New Market	12
Barbee	6
Somerville	3

Carters	5
Moss	5
Mitchell	12
Curls	7
Greens	10
Dickeys	8
Mammoth Cave	9
	---
	130 miles.

FROM GLASGOW TO MAMMOTH CAVE, via

Dickeys　　　　　　18 miles.

FROM NASHVILLE TO MAMMOTH CAVE.

Gees	9 miles.
Tyree Springs	13
Buntons	12
Franklin	10
Bowling Green	20
Pattersons	12
Dripping Springs	3
Mammoth Cave	8
	--
	87 miles.

FROM BARDSTOWN TO MAMMOTH CAVE.

New Haven	15 miles.
McDougals	10
McAchran (Cobb's stand)	12
Bear Wallow	20
Dickeys (Prewett's Knob)	7
Mammoth Cave	9
	--
	73 miles.

FROM BARDSTOWN TO MAMMOTH CAVE, via. MUNFORDSVILLE.

McAchran (Cobb's stand)	37 miles.
Munfordsville	12
Mammoth Cave	14-1/2

	63-1/2 miles.

FROM GLASGOW TO MAMMOTH CAVE, via.

Bells	18 miles.

CHAPTER I.

Mammoth Cave--Where Situated--Green River--Improved Navigation--Range of Highlands--Beautiful Woodlands--Hotel--Romantic Dell--Mouth of the Cave--Coldness of the Air--Lamps Lighted--Bones of a Giant--Violence of the Wind--Lamps Extinguished--Temperature of the Cave--Lamps Lighted--First Hoppers--Grand Vestibule--Glowing Description--Audubon Avenue--Little Bat Room--Pit Two-Hundred and Eighty Feet Deep--Main Cave--Kentucky Cliffs--The Church--Second Hoppers--Extent of the Saltpetre Manufacture in 1814.

The Mammoth Cave is situated in the County of Edmondson and State of Kentucky, equidistant from the cities of Louisville and Nashville, (about ninety miles from each,) and immediately upon the nearest road between those two places. Green River is within half a mile of the Cave, and since the improvements in its navigation, by the construction of locks and dams, steamboats can, at all seasons, ascend to Bowling Green, distant but twenty-two miles, and, for the greater part of the year, to the Cave itself.

In going to the Cave from Munfordsville, you will observe a lofty range of barren highlands to the North, which approaches nearer and nearer the Cave as you advance, until it reaches to within a mile of it. This range of highlands or cliffs, composed of calcareous rock, pursuing its rectilinear course, is seen the greater part of the way as you proceed on towards Bowling Green; and, at last, looses itself in the counties below. Under this extensive range of cliffs it is conjectured that the great subterranean territory mainly extends itself.

For a distance of two miles from the Cave, as you approach it from the South-East, the country is level. It was, until recently, a prairie, on which, however, the oak, chestnut and hickory are now growing; and having no underbrush, its smooth, verdant openings present, here and there, no unapt resemblance to the parks of the English nobility.

Emerging from these beautiful woodlands, you suddenly have a view of the hotel and adjacent grounds, which is truly lovely and picturesque. The hotel is a large edifice, two hundred feet long by forty-five wide, with piazzas, sixteen feet wide, extending the whole length of the building, both above and below, well furnished, and kept in a style, by Mr. Miller, that cannot fail to please the most fastidious epicure.

The Cave is about two-hundred yards from the hotel, and you proceed to it down a lovely and romantic dell, rendered umbrageous by a forest of trees and grape vines; and passing by the ruins of saltpetre furnaces and large mounds of ashes, you turn abruptly to the right and behold the mouth of the great cavern and as suddenly feel the coldness of its air.

It is an appalling spectacle,--how dark, how dismal, how dreary. Descending some thirty feet down rather rude steps of stone, you are fairly under the arch of this "nether world"--before you, in looking outwards, is seen a small stream of water falling from the face of the crowning rock, with a wild faltering sound, upon the ruins below, and disappearing in a deep pit,--behind you, all is gloom and darkness!

Let us now follow the guide--who, placing on his back a canteen of oil, lights the lamps, and giving one to each person, we commence our subterranean journey; having determined to confine ourselves, for this day, to an examination of *some* of the avenues on this side of the rivers, and to resume, on a future occasion, our visit to the fairy scenes beyond. I emphasize the word *some* of the avenues, because no visitor has ever yet seen one in twenty; and, although I shall attempt to describe only a few of them, and in so doing will endeavor to represent things as I saw them, and as they impressed me, I am not the less apprehensive that my descriptions will appear as unbounded exaggerations, so wonderfully vast is the Cave, so singular its formations, and so unique its characteristics.

At the place where our lamps were lighted, are to be seen the wooden pipes which conducted the water, as it fell from the ceiling, to the vats or saltpetre hoppers; and near this spot too, are interred the bones of a ***giant***, of such vast size is the skeleton, at least of such portions of it as remain. With regard to this giant, or more properly skeleton, it may be well to state, that it was found by the saltpetre workers far within the Cave years ago, and was buried by their employer where it now lies, to quiet their superstitious fears, not however before it was bereft of its head by some fearless antiquary.

Proceeding onward about one-hundred feet, we reached a door, set in a rough stone wall, stretched across and completely blocking up the Cave; which was no sooner opened, than our lamps were extinguished by the violence of the wind rushing outwards. An accurate estimate of the external temperature, may at any time, be made, by noting the force of the wind as it blows inward or outward. When it is very warm without, the wind blows outwards with violence; but when cold, it blows inwards with proportionate force. The temperature of the Cave, (winter and summer,) is invariably the same--59 deg. Fahrenheit; and its atmosphere is perfectly uniform, dry, and of most extraordinary salubrity.

Our lamps being relighted, we soon reached a narrow passage faced on the left side by a wall, built by the miners to confine the loose stone thrown up in the course of their operations, when gradually descending a short distance, we entered the great vestibule or ante-chamber of the Cave. What do we now see? Midnight!--the blackness of darkness!--Nothing! Where is the wall we were lately elbowing out of the way? It has vanished!--It is lost! We are walled in by darkness, and darkness canopies us above. Look again;--Swing your torches aloft! Aye, now you can see it; far up, a hundred feet above your head, a grey ceiling rolling dimly away like a cloud, and heavy buttresses, bending under the weight, curling and toppling over their base, begin to project their enormous masses from the shadowy wall. How vast! How solemn! How awful! The little bells of the brain are ringing in your ears; you hear nothing else--not even a sigh of air--not even the echo of a drop of water falling from the roof. The guide triumphs in your look of amazement and awe; he falls to work on certain old wooden ruins, to you, yet invisible, and builds a brace or two of fires, by the aid of which you begin to have a better conception of the scene around you. You are in the vestibule or ante-chamber, to which the spacious entrance of the Cave, and the narrow passage that succeeds it, should be considered the mere gate-way and covered approach. It is a basilica of an oval figure--two-hundred feet in length by one-hundred and fifty wide, with a roof which is as flat and level as if finished by the trowel of the plasterer, of fifty or sixty or even more feet in height. Two passages, each a hundred feet in width, open into it at its opposite extremities, but at right angles to each other; and as they preserve a straight course for five or six-hundred feet, with the same flat roof common to each, the appearance to the eye, is that of a vast hall in the shape of the letter L expanded at the angle, both branches being five-hundred feet long by one-hundred wide. The passage to the right hand is the "Great Bat Room;" (Audubon Avenue.) That in the front, the beginning of the Grand Gallery, or the Main Cavern itself. The whole of this prodigious space is covered by a single rock, in which the eye can detect no break or interruption, save at its borders, where is a broad, sweeping cornice, traced in horizontal panel-work, exceedingly noble and regular; and not a single pier or pillar of any kind contributes to support it. It needs no support. It is like the arched and ponderous roof of the poet's mausoleum:

"By its own weight made stedfast and immoveable."

The floor is very irregularly broken, consisting of vast heaps of the nitrous earth, and of the ruins of the hoppers or vats, composed of heavy planking, in which the miners were accustomed to leach it. The hall was, in fact, one of their chief factory rooms. Before their day, it was a cemetery; and here they disinterred many a mouldering skeleton, belonging it seems, to that gigantic eight or nine feet race of men of past days, whose jaw-bones so many vivacious persons have clapped over their own, like horse-collars, without laying by a single one to convince the soul of scepticism.

Such is the vestibule of the Mammoth Cave,--a hall which hundreds of visitors have passed through without being conscious of its existence. The path, leading into the Grand Gallery, hugs the wall on the left hand; and is, besides, in a hollow, flanked on the right hand by lofty mounds of earth, which the visitor, if he looks at them at all, which he will scarcely do, at so early a period after entering, will readily suppose to be the opposite walls. Those who enter the Great Bat Room, (Audubon Avenue,) into which flying visitors are seldom conducted, will indeed have some faint suspicion, for a moment, that they are passing through infinite space; but the walls of the Cave being so dark as to reflect not one single ray of light from the dim torches, and a greater number of them being necessary to disperse the gloom than are usually employed, they will still remain in ignorance of the grandeur around them.

Such is the vestibule of the Mammoth Cave, as described by the ingenious author of "Calavar," "Peter Pilgrim," &c.

From the vestibule we entered Audubon Avenue, which is more than a mile long, fifty or sixty feet wide and as many high. The roof or ceiling exhibits, as you walk along, the appearance of floating clouds--and such is observable in many other parts of the Cave. Near the termination of this avenue, a natural well, twenty-five feet deep, and containing the purest water, has been recently discovered; it is surrounded by stalagmite columns, extending from the floor to the roof, upon the incrustations of which, when lights are suspended, the reflection from the water below and the various objects above and around, gives to the whole scene an appearance equally rare and picturesque. This spot, however, being difficult of access, is but seldom visited.

The Little Bat Room Cave--a branch of Audubon Avenue,--is on the left as you advance, and not more than three-hundred yards from the great vestibule. It is but little more than a quarter of a mile in length, and is remarkable for its pit of two-hundred and eighty feet in depth; and as being the hibernal resort of bats. Tens of thousands of them are seen hanging from the walls, in apparently a torpid state, during the winter, but no sooner does the spring open, than they disappear.

Returning from the Little Bat Room and Audubon Avenue, we pass again through the vestibule, and enter the Main Cave or Grand Gallery. This is a vast tunnel extending for miles, averaging throughout, fifty feet in width by as many in height It is truly a noble subterranean avenue; the largest of which man has any knowledge, and replete with interest, from its varied characteristics and majestic grandeur.

Proceeding down the main Cave about a quarter of a mile, we came to the Kentucky Cliffs, so called from the fancied resemblance to the cliffs on the Kentucky River, and descending gradually about twenty feet entered the church, when our guide was discovered in the ***pulpit*** fifteen feet above us, having reached there by a gallery which leads from the cliffs. The ceiling here is sixty three feet high, and the church itself, including the recess, cannot be less than one hundred feet in diameter. Eight or ten feet above and immediately behind the pulpit, is the organ loft, which is sufficiently capacious for an. organ and choir of the largest size. There would appear to be something like design in all this;--here is a church large enough to accomodate thousands, a solid projection of the wall of the Cave to serve as a pulpit, and a few feet back a place for an organ and choir. In this great temple of nature, religious service has been frequently held, and it requires but a slight effort on the part of a speaker, to make himself distinctly heard by the largest congregation.

Sometimes the guides climb up the high and ragged sides, and suspend lamps in the crevices and on the projections of the rock, thus lighting up a scene of wild grandeur and sublimity.

Concerts too have been held here, and the melody of song has been heard, such as would delight the ear of a Catalini or a Malibran.

Leaving the church you will observe, on ascending, a large embankment of lixiviated earth thrown out by the miners more than thirty years ago, the print of wagon wheels and the tracks of oxen, as distinctly defined as though they were made but yesterday; and continuing on for a short distance, you arrive at the Second Hoppers. Here are seen the ruins of the old nitre works, leaching vats, pump frames and two lines of wooden pipes; one to lead fresh water from the dripping spring to the vats filled with the nitrous earth, and the other to convey the lye drawn from the large reservoir, back to the furnace at the mouth of the Cave.

The quantity of nitrous earth contained in the Cave is "sufficient to supply the whole population of the globe with saltpetre."

"The dirt gives from three to five pounds of nitrate of lime to the bushel, requiring a large proportion of fixed alkali to produce the required crystalization, and when left in the Cave become re-impregnated in three years. When saltpetre bore a high price, immense quantities were manufactured at the Mammoth Cave, but the return of peace brought the saltpetre from the East Indies in competition with the American, and drove that of the produce of our country entirely from the market. An idea may be formed of the extent of the manufacture of saltpetre at this Cave, from the fact that the contract for the supply of the fixed alkali alone for the Cave, for the year 1814, was twenty thousand dollars."

"The price of the article was so high, and the profits of the manufacturer so great, as to set half the western world gadding after nitre caves--the gold mines of the day. Cave hunting in fact became a kind of mania, beginning with speculators, and ending with hair brained young men, who dared for the love of adventure the risk which others ran for profit." Every hole, remarked an old miner, the size of a man's body, has been penetrated for miles around the Mammoth Cave, but although we found "*petre earth*," we never could find a cave worth having.

CHAPTER II.

Gothic Gallery--Gothic Avenue--Good Road--Mummies--Interesting Account of Them--Gothic Avenue once called Haunted Chamber--Why so Named-- Adventure of a Miner in Former Days.

In looking from the ruins of the nitre works, to the left and some thirty feet above, you will see a large cave, connected with which is a narrow gallery sweeping across the Main Cave and losing itself in a cave, which is seen above to your right This latter cave is the Gothic Avenue, which no doubt was at one time connected with the cave opposite and on the same level, forming a complete bridge over the main avenue, but afterwards broken down and separated by some great convulsion.

The cave on the left, which is filled with sand, has been penetrated but a short distance; still from its great size at its entrance, it is more than probable, that, were all obstructions removed, it might be found to extend for miles.

While examining the old saltpetre works, the guide left us without our being aware of it, but casting our eyes around we perceived him standing some forty feet above, on the projection of a huge rock, or tower, which commands a view of the grand gallery to a great extent both up and down.

Leaving the Main Cave and ascending a flight of stairs twenty or thirty feet, we entered the Gothic Avenue, so named from the Gothic appearance of some of its compartments. This avenue is about forty feet wide, fifteen feet high and two miles long. The ceiling looks in many places as smooth and white as though it had been under the trowel of the most skilful plasterer. A good road has been made throughout this cave, and such is the temperature and purity of its atmosphere, that every visitor must experience their salutary influences.

In a recess on the left hand elevated a few feet above the floor and about fifty feet from the head of the stairs leading up from the Main Avenue, two mummies long since taken away, were to be seen in 1813. They were in good preservation; one was a female with her extensive wardrobe placed before her. The removal of those mummies from the place in which they were found can be viewed as little less than sacrilege. There they had been, perhaps for centuries, and there they ought to have been left. What has become of them I know not. One of them, it is said, was lost in the burning of the Cincinnati museum. The wardrobe of the female was given to a Mr. Ward, of Massachusetts, who I believe presented it to the British Museum.

Two of the miners found a mummy in Audubon Avenue, in 1814. With a view to conceal it for a time, they placed large stones over it, and marked the walls about the spot so that they might find it at some future period; this however, they were never able to effect. In 1840, the present hotel keeper Mr. Miller, learning the above facts, went in search of the place designated, taking with him very many lights, and found the marks on the walls, and near to them the mummy. It was, however, so much injured and broken to pieces by the heavy weights which had been placed upon it, as to be of little interest or value. I have no doubt, that if proper efforts were made, mummies and other objects of curiosity might be found, which would tend to throw light on the early history of the first inhabitants of this continent.

Believing, that whatever may relate to these mummies cannot fail to interest, I will extract from the recently published narrative of a highly scientific gentleman of New York, himself one of the early visitors to the Cave.

"On my first visit to the Mammoth Cave in 1813, I saw a relic of ancient times, which requires a minute description. This description is from a memorandum made in the Cave at the time.

"In the digging of saltpetre earth, in the short cave, a flat rock was met with by the workmen, a little below the surface of the earth in the Cave; this stone was raised, and was about four feet wide and as many long; beneath it was a square excavation about three feet deep and as many in length and width. In this small nether subterranean chamber, sat in solemn silence one of the human species, a female with her wardrobe and ornaments placed at her side. The body was in a state of perfect preservation, and sitting erect The arms were folded up and the hands were laid across the bosom; around the two wrists was wound a small cord, designed probably, to keep them in the posture in which they were first placed;

around the body and next thereto, was wrapped two deer-skins. These skins appear to have been dressed in some mode different from what is now practised by any people, of whom I have any knowledge. The hair of the skins was cut off very near the surface. The skins were ornamented with the imprints of vines and leaves, which were sketched with a substance perfectly white. Outside of these two skins was a large square sheet, which was either wove or knit. This fabric was the inner bark of a tree, which I judge from appearances to be that of the linn tree. In its texture and appearance, it resembled the South Sea Island cloth or matting; this sheet enveloped the whole body and the head. The hair on the head was cut off within an eighth of an inch of the skin, except near the neck, where it was an inch long. The color of the hair was a dark red; the teeth were white and perfect. I discovered no blemish upon the body, except a wound between two ribs near the back-bone; one of the eyes had also been injured. The finger and toe nails were perfect and quite long. The features were regular. I measured the length of one of the bones of the arm with a string, from the elbow to the wrist joint, and they equalled my own in length, viz: ten and a half inches. From the examination of the whole frame, I judged the figure to be that of a very tall female, say five feet ten inches in height. The body, at the time it was first discovered, weighed but fourteen pounds, and was perfectly dry; on exposure to the atmosphere, it gained in weight by absorbing dampness four pounds. Many persons have expressed surprise that a human body of great size should weigh so little, as many human skeletons of nothing but bone, exceed this weight. Recently some experiments have been made in Paris, which have demonstrated the fact of the human body being reduced to ten pounds, by being exposed to a heated atmosphere for a long period of time. The color of the skin was dark, not black; the flesh was hard and dry upon the bones. At the side of the body lay a pair of moccasins, a knapsack and an indispensable or reticule. I will describe these in the order in which I have named them. The moccasins were made of wove or knit bark, like the wrapper I have described. Around the top there was a border to add strength and perhaps as an ornament. These were of middling size, denoting feet of small size. The shape of the moccasins differs but little from the deer-skin moccasins worn by the Northern Indians. The knapsack was of wove or knit bark, with a deep, strong border around the top, and was about the size of knapsacks used by soldiers. The workmanship of it was neat, and such as would do credit as a fabric, to a manufacturer of the present day. The reticule was also made of knit or wove bark. The shape was much like a horseman's valise, opening its whole length on the top. On the side of the opening and a few inches from it, were two rows of hoops, one row on each side. Two cords were fastened to one end of the reticule at the top, which passed through the loop on one side and then on the other side, the whole length, by which it was laced up and secured. The edges of the top of the reticule were strengthened with deep fancy borders. The articles contained in the knapsack and reticule were quite numerous, and are as follows: one head cap, made of wove or knit bark, without any border, and of the shape of the plainest night cap; seven head-dresses made of the quills of large birds, and put together somewhat in the same way that feather fans are made, except that the pipes of the quills are not drawn to a point, but are spread out in straight lines with the top. This was done by perforating the pipe of the quill in two places and running two cords through these holes, and then winding around the quills and the cord, fine thread, to fasten each quill in the place designed for it. These cords extended some length beyond the quills on each side, so that on placing the feathers erect on the head, the cords could be tied together at the back of the head. This would enable the wearer to present a beautiful display of feathers standing erect and extending a distance above the head, and entirely surrounding it. These were most splendid head dresses, and would be a magnificent ornament to the head of a female at the present day,--several hundred strings of beads; these consisted of very hard brown seed smaller than hemp seed, in each of which a small hole had been made, and through this hole a small three corded thread, similar in appearance and texture to seine twine; these were tied up in bunches, as a merchant ties up coral beads when he exposes them for sale. The red hoofs of fawns, on a string supposed to be worn around the neck as a necklace. These hoofs were about twenty in number, and may have been emblematic of Innocence; the claw of an eagle, with a hole made in it, through which a cord was passed, so that it could be worn pendent from the neck; the jaw of a bear designed to be worn in the same manner as the eagle's claw, and supplied with a cord to suspend it around the neck; two rattlesnake-skins, one of these had fourteen rattles upon it, these were neatly folded up; some vegetable colors done up in leaves; a small bunch of deer sinews, resembling cat-gut in appearance; several bunches of thread and twine, two and three threaded, some of which were nearly white; seven needles, some of these were of horn and some of bone, they were smooth and appeared to have been much used. These needles had each a knob or whirl on the top, and at the other end were brought to a point like a large sail needle. They had no eyelets to receive a thread. The top of one of these needles was handsomely scalloped; a hand-piece made of deer-skin, with a hole through it for the thumb, and designed probably to protect the hand in the use of the needle, the same as thimbles are now used; two whistles about eight inches long made of cane, with a joint about one third the length; over the joint is an opening extending to each side of the tube of the whistle, these openings were about three-fourths of an inch long and a quarter of an inch wide, and had each a flat reed placed in the opening. These whistles were tied together with a cord wound around them.

"I have been thus minute in describing the mute witness from the days of other times, and the articles which were deposited within her earthen house. Of the race of people to whom she belonged when living, we know nothing; and as to conjecture, the reader who gathers from these pages this account, can judge of the matter as well as those who saw the remnant of mortality in the subterranean chambers in which she was entombed. The cause of the preservation of her body, dress and ornaments is no mystery. The dry atmosphere of the Cave, with the nitrate of lime, with which the earth that covers the bottom of these nether palaces is so highly impregnated, preserves animal flesh, and it will neither putrify nor decompose when confined to its unchanging action. Heat and moisture are both absent from the Cave, and it is these two agents, acting together, which produce both animal and vegetable decomposition and putrefaction.

"In the ornaments, etc., of this mute witness of ages gone, we have a record of olden time, from which, in the absence of a written record, we may draw some conclusions. In the various articles which constituted her ornaments, there were no metallic substances. In the make of her dress, there is no evidence of the use of any other machinery than the bone and horn needles. The beads are of a substance, of the use of which for such purposes, we have no account among people of whom we have any written record. She had no warlike arms. By what process the hair upon her head was cut short, or by what process the deer-skins were shorn, we have no means of conjecture. These articles afford us the same means of judging of the nation to which she belonged, and of their advances in the arts, that future generations will have in the exhumation of a tenant of one of our modern tombs, with the funeral shroud, etc. in a state of like preservation; with this difference, that with the present inhabitants of this section of the globe, but few articles of ornament are deposited with the body. The features of this ancient member of the human family much resembled those of a tall, handsome American woman. The forehead was high, and the head well formed.

"Ye mouldering relics of a race departed,   Your names have perished; not a trace remains."

The Gothic Avenue was once called the Haunted Chamber, and owed its name to an adventure that befell one of the miners in former days, which is thus related by the author of "Calavar."

In the Lower Branch is a room called the Salts Room, which produces considerable quantities of the sulphate of magnesia, or of soda, we forget which--a mineral that the proprietor of the Cave did not fail to turn to account. The miner in question was a new and raw hand--of course neither very well acquainted with the Cave itself, nor with the approved modes of averting or repairing accidents, to which, from the nature of their occupation, the miners were greatly exposed. Having been sent, one day, in charge of an older workman, to the Salts Room to dig a few sacks of the salt, and finding that the path to this sequestered nook was perfectly plain; and that, from the Haunted Chambers being a single, continuous passage without branches, it was impossible to wander from it, our hero disdained on his second visit, to seek or accept assistance, and trudged off to his work alone. The circumstance being common enough he was speedily forgotten by his brother miners; and it was not until several hours after, when they all left off their toil for the more agreeable duty of eating their dinner, that his absence was remarked, and his heroical resolution to make his way alone to the Salts Room remembered. As it was apparent, from the time he had been gone, that some accident must have happened to him, half a dozen men, most of them negroes, stripped half naked, their usual working costume, were sent to hunt him up, a task supposed to be of no great difficulty, unless he had fallen into a pit. In the meanwhile, the poor miner, it seems, had succeeded in reaching the Salts Room, filling his sack, and retracing his steps half way back to the Grand Gallery; when finding the distance greater than he thought it ought to be, the conceit entered his unlucky brain that he *might* perhaps be going wrong.

No sooner had the suspicion struck him, than he fell into a violent terror, dropped his sack, ran backwards, then returned, then ran back again--each time more frightened and bewildered than before; until at last he ended his adventure by tumbling over a stone and extinguishing his lamp. Thus left in the dark, not knowing where to turn, frightened out of his wits besides, he fell to remembering his sins--always remembered by those who are lost in the Cave--and praying with all his might for succor. But hours passed away, and assistance came not; the poor fellow's frenzy increased; he felt himself a doomed man; he thought his terrible situation was a judgment imposed on him for his wickedness; nay, he even believed, at last, that he was no longer an inhabitant of the earth--that he had been translated, even in the body, to the place of torment--in other words, that he was in hell itself, the prey of the devils, who would presently be let loose upon him. It was at this moment the miners in search of him made their appearance; they lighted upon his sack, lying where he had thrown it, and set up a great shout, which was the first intimation he had of their approach. He started up, and seeing them in the distance, the half naked negroes in advance, all swinging their torches aloft, he, not doubting they were those identical devils whose appearance he had been expecting, took to his heels, yelling lustily for mercy; nor did he stop, notwithstanding the calls of his amazed friends, until he had fallen a second time over the rocks, where he lay on his face, roaring for pity, until, by dint of much pulling and shaking, he was convinced that he was still in the world and the Mammoth Cave. Such is the story of the Haunted Chambers, the name having been given to commemorate the incident.

CHAPTER III.

Stalagmite Pillars--The Bell--Vulcan's Furnace--Register Rooms-- Stalagmite Hall or Gothic Chapel--Devil's Arm-Chair--Elephant's Head--Lover's Leap--Napoleon's Dome--Salts Cave--Annetti's Dome.

Resuming our explorations in this most interesting avenue, we soon came in sight of stalagmite pillars, reaching from the floor to the ceiling, once perhaps white and translucent, but now black and begrimed with smoke. At this point we were startled by the hollow tread of our feet, caused by the proximity of another large avenue underneath, which the guide assured us he had often visited. In this neighborhood too, there are a number of Stalactites, one of which was called the Bell, which on being struck, sounded like the deep bell of a cathedral; but it now no longer tolls, having been broken in twain by a visiter from Philadelphia some years ago. Further on our way, we passed Louisa's Bower and Vulcan's Furnace, where there is a heap, not unlike cinders in appearance, and some dark colored water, in which I suppose the great forger used to slake his iron and perhaps his bolts. Next in order and not very distant are the new and old Register Rooms. Here on the ceiling which is as smooth and white as if it had been finished off by the plasterer, thousands of names have been traced by the smoke of a candle--names which can create no pleasing associations or recollections; names unknown to fame, and which might excite disgust, when read for the first time on the ceiling which they have disfigured.

Soon after leaving the old Register Room, we were halted by our guide, who took from us all the lamps excepting one. Having made certain arrangements, he cried aloud, "Come on!" which we did, and in a few moments entered an apartment of surprising grandeur and magnificence. This apartment or hall is elliptical in shape and eighty feet long by fifty wide. Stalagmite columns, of vast size nearly block up the two ends; and two rows of pillars of smaller dimensions, reaching from floor to ceiling and equidistant from the wall on either side, extend its entire length. Against the pillars, and in many places from the ceiling, our lamps were hanging, and, lighting up the whole space, exhibited to our enraptured sight a scene surpassingly grand, and well calculated to inspire feelings of solemnity and awe. This is the Stalagmite Hall, or as some call it, the Gothic Chapel, which no one can see under such circumstances as did our party, without being forcibly reminded of the old, very old cathedrals of Europe. Continuing our walk we came to the Devil's Arm-Chair. This is a large Stalagmite column, in the centre of which is formed a capacious seat. Like most other visiters we seated ourselves in the chair of his Satanic Majesty, and drank sulphur water dipped up from a small basin of rock, near the foot of the chair. Further on we passed a number of Stalactites and Stalagmites, Napoleon's Breast-Work, (behind which we found ashes and burnt cane,) the Elephant's Head, the Curtain, and arrived at last at the Lover's Leap. The Lover's Leap is a large pointed rock projecting over a dark and gloomy hollow, thirty or more feet deep. Our guide told us that the young ladies often asked their beaux to take the Lover's Leap, but that he never knew any to "love hard enough" to attempt it. We descended into the hollow, immediately below the Lover's Leap, and entered to the left and at right-angle with our previous course, a passage or chasm in the rock, three feet wide and fifty feet high, which conducted us to the lower branch of the Gothic Avenue. At the entrance of this lower branch is an immensely large flat rock called Gatewood's Dining Table, to the right of which is a cave, which we penetrated, as far as the Cooling Tub--a beautiful basin of water six feet wide and three deep--into which a small stream of the purest water pours itself from the ceiling and afterwards finds its way into the Flint Pit at no great distance. Returning, we wound around Gatewood's Dining Table, which nearly blocks up the way, and continued our walk along the lower branch more than half a mile, passing Napoleon's Dome, the Cinder Banks, the Crystal Pool, the Salts Cave, etc., etc. Descending a few feet and leaving the cave which continues onwards, we entered, on our right, a place of great seclusion and grandeur, called Annetti's Dome. Through a crevice in the right wall of the dome is a waterfall. The water issues in a stream a foot in diameter, from a high cave in the side of the dome--falls upon the solid bottom, and passes off by a small channel into the Cistern, which is directly on the pathway of the cave. The

Cistern is a large pit, which is usually kept nearly full of water.

Near the end of this branch, (the lower branch) there is a crevice in the ceiling over the last spring, through which the sound of water may be heard falling in a cave or open space above.

Highly gratified with what we had now seen in the Gothic Avenue, we concluded to pursue it no further, but to retrace our steps to the Main Cave, regretting however, that we had not visited the Salts Cave, (a branch of the Gothic Avenue,) on being told, when too late, that it would have amply compensated us for our trouble, being rich in fine specimens of Epsom or Glauber salts.

CHAPTER IV.

The Ball-Room--Willie's Spring--Wandering Willie--Ox-Stalls--Giant's Coffin--Acute-Angle or Great Bend--Range of Cabins--Curative Properties of the Cave Air long known.

We are now again in the Main Cave or Grand Gallery, which continues to increase in interest as we advance, eliciting from our party frequent and loud exclamations of admiration and wonder. Not many steps from the stairs leading down from the Gothic Avenue into the Main Cave, is the Ball-Room, so called from its singular adaptedness to such a purpose; for there is an orchestra, fifteen or eighteen feet high, large enough to accommodate a hundred or more musicians, with a gallery extending back to the level of the high embankment near the Gothic Avenue; besides which, the avenue here is lofty, wide, straight and perfectly level for several hundred feet. At the trifling expense of a plank floor, seats and lamps, a ball-room might be had, if not more splendid, at all events more grand and magnificent than any other on earth. The effect of music here would be truly inspiring; but the awful solemnity of the place may, in the opinion of many, prevent its being used as a temple of Terpsichore. Extremes, we are told, often meet. The same objection has been urged against the Cave's being used for religious services. "No clergyman," remarked a distinguished divine, "be he ever so eloquent could concentrate the attention of his congregation in such a place. The God of nature speaks too loud here for ***man to be heard***."

Leaving these points to be settled as they may, we will proceed onwards; the road now is broad and fine, and in many places dusty. Next in order is Willie's Spring, a beautifully fluted niche in the left hand wall, caused by the continual attrition of water trickling down into a basin below. This spring derives its name from that of a young gentleman, the son of a highly respectable clergyman of Cincinnati, who, in the spirit of romance, assumed the name of Wandering Willie, and taking with him his violin, marched on foot to the Cave. Wishing no better place in which to pass the night, he selected this spot, requesting the guide to call for him in the morning. This he did and found him fast asleep upon his bed of earth, with his violin beside him--ever since it has been called Willie's Spring. Just beyond the spring and near the left wall, is the place where the oxen were fed during the time of the miners; and strewn around are a great many corn-cobs, to all appearance, and in fact, perfectly sound, although they have lain there for more than thirty years. In this neighborhood is a niche of great size in the wall on the left, and reaching from the roof to the bottom of a pit more than thirty feet deep, down the sides of which, water of the purest kind is continually dripping, and is afterwards conducted to a large trough, from which the invalids obtain their supply of water, during their sojourn in the Cave. Near the bottom, this pit or well expands into a large room, out of which, there is no opening. It is probable that Richardson's Spring in the Deserted Chambers is supplied from this well. Passing the Well Cave, Rocky Cave, etc., etc., we arrived at the Giant's Coffin, a huge rock on the right, thus named from its singular resemblance in shape to a coffin; its locality, apart from its great size, renders it particularly conspicuous, as all must pass around it, in leaving the Main Cave, to visit the rivers and the thousand wonders beyond. At this point commence those incrustations, which, portraying every imaginable figure on the ceiling, afford full scope to the fanciful to picture what they will, whether of "birds, or beasts, or creeping things." About a hundred yards beyond the Coffin, the Cave makes a majestic curve, and sweeping round the Great Bend or Acute-Angle, resumes its general course. Here the guide ignited a Bengal light. This vast amphitheatre became illuminated, and a scene of enchantment was exposed to our view. Poets may conceive, but no language can describe, the splendor and sublimity of the scene. The rapturous exclamations of our party might have been heard from afar, both up and down this place of wonders. Opposite to the Great Bend, is the entrance of the Sick Room Cave, so called from the fact of the sudden sickness of a visiter a few years ago, supposed to have been caused by his smoking, with others, cigars in one of its most remote and confined nooks. Immediately beyond the Great Bend, a row of cabins, built for consumptive patients, commences. All of these are framed buildings, with the exception of two, which are of stone. They stand in line, from thirty to one hundred feet apart, exhibiting a picturesque, yet at the same time, a gloomy and mournful appearance. They are well furnished, and without question, would with good and comfortable accommodations, pure air and uniform temperature, cure the pulmonary consumption. The invalids in the Cave ought to be cured; but I doubt whether the Cave air or any thing else can cure confirmed Phthisis. A knowledge of the curative properties of the Cave air, is not, as is generally supposed, of recent date. It has been long known. A physician of great respectability, formerly a member of Congress from the district adjoining the Cave, was so firmly convinced of the medical properties of its air, as to express more than twenty years ago, as his opinion, that the State of Kentucky ought to purchase it, with a view to establish a hospital in one of its avenues. Again the author of "Calavar," himself a distinguished professor of medicine, makes the following remarks in relation to the Cave air, as far back as 1832, the date of his visit:

"It is always temperate. Its purity, judging from its effects on the lungs, and from other circumstances, is remarkable, though in what its purity consists, I know not. But, be its composition what it may, it is certain its effects upon the spirits and bodily powers of visiters, are extremely exhilarating; and that it is not less salubrious than enlivening. The nitre diggers were a famously healthy set of men; it was a common and humane practice to employ laborers of enfeebled constitutions, who were soon restored to health and strength, though kept at constant labour; and more joyous, merry fellows were never seen. The oxen, of which several were kept day and night in the Cave, hauling the nitrous earth, were after a month or two of toil, in as fine condition for the shambles, as if fattened in the stall. The ordinary visiter, though rambling a dozen hours or more, over paths of the roughest and most difficult kind, is seldom conscious of fatigue, until he returns to the upper air; and then it seems to him, at least in the summer season, that he has exchanged the atmosphere of paradise for that of a charnel warmed by steam--all without is so heavy, so dank, so dead, so mephitic. Awe and even apprehension, if that has been felt, soon yield to the influence of the delicious air of the Cave; and after a time a certain jocund feeling is found mingled with the deepest impressions of sublimity, which there are so many objects to awaken. I recommend all broken hearted lovers and dyspeptic dandies to carry their complaints to the Mammoth Cave, where they will undoubtedly find themselves "translated" into very buxom and happy persons before they are aware of it."

CHAPTER V.

Star Chamber--Salts Room--Indian Houses--Cross Rooms--Black Chambers-- A Dinner Party--Humble Chute--Solitary Care--Fairy Grotto--Chief City or Temple--Lee's Description--Return to the Hotel.

The Star Chamber next attracted our attention. It presents the most perfect optical illusion imaginable; in looking up to the ceiling, which is here very high, you seem to see the very firmament itself, studded with stars; and afar off, a comet with its long, bright tail. Not far from this Star Chamber, may be seen, in a cavity in the wall on the right, and about twenty feet above the floor, an oak pole about ten feet long and six inches in diameter, with two round sticks of half the thickness and three feet long, tied on to it transversely, at about four feet apart. By means of a ladder we ascended to the cavity, and found the pole to be firmly fixed--one end resting on the bottom of the cavity, and the other reaching across and forced into a crevice about three feet above. We supposed that this was a ladder once used by the former inhabitants of the Cave, in getting the salts which are incrusted on the walls in many places. Doct. Locke, of the Medical College of Ohio, is, however, of the opinion, that on it was placed a dead body,--similar contrivances being used by some Indian tribes on which to place their dead. Although thousands have passed the spot, still this was never seen until the fall of 1841. Ages have doubtless rolled by since this was placed here, and yet it is perfectly sound; even the bark which confines the transverse pieces shows no marks of decay.

We passed through some Side Cuts, as they are called. These are caves opening on the sides of the avenues; and after running for some distance, entering them again. Some of them exceed half a mile in length; but most generally they are short. In many of them, "quartz, calcedony, red ochre, gypsum, and salts are found." The walking, in this part of the avenue, being rough, we progressed but slowly, until we reached the Salts Room; here we found the walls and ceiling covered with salts hanging in crystals. The least agitation of the air causing flakes of the crystals to fall like snow. In the Salts Room are the Indian houses, under the rocks--small spaces or rooms completely covered--some of which contain ashes and cane partly burnt. The **Cross Rooms**, which we next come to, is a grand section of this avenue; the ceiling has an unbroken span of one hundred and seventy feet, without a column to support it! The mouths of two caves are seen from this point, neither of which we visited, and much to our loss, as will appear from the following extract from the "Notes on the Mammoth Cave, by E.F. Lee, Esq., Civil Engineer," in relation to one of them--the Black Chambers:

"At the ruins in the Black Chambers, there are a great many large blocks composed of different strata of rocks, cemented together, resembling the walls, pedestals, cornices, etc., of some old castle, scattered over the bottom of the Cave. The avenue here is so wide, as to make it quite a task to walk from one side to the other. On the right hand, beyond the ruins, you enter the right branch, on the same level--the ceiling of which is regularly arched. Through the Big Chimneys you ascend into an upper room, about the size of the Main Cave, the bottom of which is higher than the ceiling of the one below. Proceeding on we soon heard the low murmurings of a water-fall,--the sound of which becomes louder and louder as we advanced, until we reached the Cataract. In the roof are perforations as large as a hogshead, on the right hand side, from which water is ever falling, on ordinary occasions in not very large quantities; but after heavy rains--in torrents; and with a horrible roar that shakes the walls and resounds afar through the Cave. It is at such times that these cascades are worthy the name of cataracts, which they bear. The water falling into a great funnel-shaped pit, immediately vanishes."

Here we concluded to dine, and at quite a fashionable hour--4, P.M. The guide arranged the plates, knives and forks, wine-glasses, etc., on a huge table of rock, and announced,--"Dinner is ready!" We filled our plates with the excellent viands prepared at the Cave House, and seating ourselves on the rocks or nitre earth, partook of our repast with the gusto of gourmands, and quaffing, ever and anon, wines which would have done credit to the Astor or Tremont House. "There may be," remarked our corpulent friend B., "a great deal of romance in this way of eating--with your plate on your lap, and seated on a rock or a lump of nitre earth--but for my part I would rather dispense with the poetry of the thing and eat a good dinner, whether above or below ground, from off a bona-fide table, and seated in a good substantial chair. The proprietor ought to have at all the watering places, (and they are numerous,) tables, chairs, and the necessary table furniture, that visitors might partake of their collations in some degree of comfort." The guide who, by the way, is a very intelligent and facetious fellow, was much amused at the suggestion of our friend, and remarked that "the owner of the Cave, Doct. Croghan, lived near Louisville, and that the only way to get such '*fixings*' at the watering places, was to write to him on the subject." "Then," said B., "for the sake of those who may follow after us, I will take it upon myself to write."

From this point you have a view of the Main Avenue on our left, pursuing its general course, and exhibiting the same solemn grandeur as from the commencement,--and directly before us the way to the Humble Chute and the Cataract. The Humble Chute is the entrance to the Solitary Chambers; before entering which, we must crawl on our hands and knees some fifteen or twenty feet under a low arch. It is appropriately named; as is the Solitary Chambers which we have now entered. You feel here,--to use an expression of one of our party,--"out of the world." Without dwelling on the intervening objects--although they are numerous and not without interest,--we will enter at once the Fairy Grotto of the Solitary Cave. It is in truth a fairy grotto; a countless number of Stalactites are seen extending, at irregular distances, from the roof to the floor, of various sizes and of the most fantastic shapes--some quite straight, some crooked, some large and hollow--forming irregularly fluted columns; and some solid near the ceiling, and divided lower down, into a great number of small branches like the roots of trees; exhibiting the appearance of a coral grove. Hanging our lamps to the incrustations on the columns, the grove of Stalactites became faintly lighted up, disclosing a scene of extraordinary wildness and beauty. "This is nothing to what you'll see on the other side of the rivers," cries our guide, smiling at our enthusiastic admiration. With all its present beauty, this grotto is far from being what it was, before it was despoiled and robbed some eight or nine years ago, by a set of vandals, who, through sheer wantonness, broke many of the stalactites, leaving them strewn on the floor--a disgustful memorial of their vulgar propensities and barbarian-like conduct.

Returning from the Fairy Grotto, we entered the Main Cave at the Cataract, and continued our walk to the Chief City or Temple, which is thus described by Lee, in his "Notes on the Mammoth Cave:"

"The Temple is an immense vault covering an area of two acres, and covered by a single dome of solid rock, one hundred and twenty feet high. It excels in size the Cave of Staffa; and rivals the celebrated vault in the Grotto of Antiparos, which is said to be the largest in the world. In passing through from one end to the other, the dome appears to follow like the sky in passing from place to place on the earth. In the middle of the dome there is a large mound of rocks rising on one side nearly to the top, very steep and forming what is called the **Mountain**. When first I ascended this mound from the cave below, I was struck with a feeling of awe more deep and intense, than any thing that I had ever before experienced. I could only observe the narrow circle which was illuminated immediately around me; above and beyond was apparently an unlimited space, in which the ear could catch not the slightest sound, nor the eye find an object to rest upon. It was filled with silence and darkness; and yet I knew that I was beneath the earth, and that this space, however large it might be, was actually bounded by solid walls. My curiosity was rather excited than gratified. In order that I might see the whole in one connected view, I built fires in many places with the pieces of cane which I found scattered among the rocks. Then taking my stand on the Mountain, a scene was presented of surprising magnificence. On the opposite side the strata of gray limestone, breaking up by steps from the bottom, could scarcely be discerned in the distance by the glimmering light. Above was the lofty dome, closed at the top by a smooth oval slab, beautifully defined in the outline, from which the walls sloped away on the right and left into thick darkness. Every one has heard of the dome of the Mosque of St. Sophia, of St. Peter's and St. Paul's; they are never spoken of but in terms of admiration, as the chief works of architecture, and among the noblest and most stupendous examples of what man can do when aided by science; and yet when compared with the dome of this Temple, they sink into comparative insignificance. Such is the surpassing grandeur of Nature's works."

To us, the Temple seemed to merit the glowing description above given, but what would Lee think, on being told, that since the discovery of the rivers and the world of beauties beyond them, not one person in fifty visits the Temple or the Fairy Grotto; they are now looked upon as tame and uninteresting. The hour being now late, we concluded to proceed no further, but to return to the hotel, where we arrived at 11, P.M.

CHAPTER VI.

Arrival of a large Party--Second Visit--Lamps Extinguished--Laughable Confusion--Wooden Bowl--Deserted Chambers--Richardson's Side-Saddle Pit--The Labyrinth--Louisa's Dome--Gorin's Dome--Bottomless Pit-- Separation of our Party.

On being summoned to breakfast the next morning, we ascertained that a large party of ladies and gentlemen had arrived during our absence, who, like ourselves, were prepared to enter the Cave. They, however, were for hurrying over the rivers, to the distant points beyond--we, for examining leisurely the avenues on this side. At 8 o'clock, both parties accompanied by their respective guides and making a very formidable array, set out from the hotel, happy in the anticipation of the "sights to be seen." It was amusing to hear the remarks, and to witness the horror of some of the party on first beholding the mouth of the Cave. Oh! it is so frightful!--It is so cold!--I **cannot** go in! Notwithstanding all this, curiosity prevailed, and down we went--arranged our lamps, which being extinguished in passing through the doorway by the strong current of air rushing outwards, there arose such a clamor, such laughter, such screaming, such crying out for the guides, as though all Bedlam had broke loose,--the guides exerting themselves to quiet apprehensions, and the visiters of yesterday knowing that there was neither danger nor just cause of alarm, doing their utmost to counteract their efforts, by well feigned exclamations of terror. At length the lamps were re-lighted and order being restored, onward we went. The Vestibule and Church were each in turn illuminated, to the enthusiastic delight of all--even those of the party, who were but now so terrified, were loud in their expressions of admiration and wonder. Arrived at the Giant's Coffin, we leave the Main Cave to enter regions very dissimilar to those we have seen. A narrow passage behind the Coffin leads to a circular room, one hundred feet in diameter, with a low roof, called the Wooden Bowl, in allusion to its figure, or as some say, from a wooden bowl having been found here by some old miner. This Bowl is the vestibule of the Deserted Chambers. On the right, are the Steeps of Time, (why so called we are left to conjecture,) down which, descending about twenty feet, and almost perpendicularly for the first ten, we enter the Deserted Chambers, which in their course present features extremely wild, terrific and multiform. For two hundred yards the ceiling as you advance is rough and broken, but further on, it is waving, white and smooth as if worn by water. At Richardson's Spring, the imprint of moccasins and of children's feet, of some by-gone age, were recently seen. There are more pits in the Deserted Chambers than in any other portion of the Cave; and among the most noted are the Covered Pit, the Side-Saddle Pit and the Bottomless Pit. Indeed the whole range of these chambers, is so interrupted by pits, and throughout is so irregular and serpentine and so bewildering from the number of its branches, that the visiter, doubtful of his footing, and uncertain as to his course, is soon made sensible of the prudence of the regulation, which enjoins him, "not to leave the guide." "The Covered Pit is in a little branch to the left; this pit is twelve or fifteen feet in diameter, covered with a thin rock, around which a narrow crevice extends, leaving only a small support on one side. There is a large rock resting on the centre of the cover. The sound of a waterfall may be heard from the pit but cannot be seen." The Side-Saddle Pit is about twenty feet long and eight feet wide, with a margin about three feet high, and extending lengthwise ten feet, against which one may safely lean, and view the interior of the pit and dome. After a short walk from this place, we came to a ladder on our right, which conducted us down about fifteen feet into a narrow pass, not more than five feet wide; this pass is the Labyrinth, one end of which leads to the Bottomless Pit, entering it about fifty feet down, and the other after various windings, now up, now down, over a bridge, and up and down ladders, conducts you to one of the chief glories of the Cave,--Gorin's Dome; which, strange to tell, was not discovered until a few years ago. Immediately behind the ladder, there is a narrow opening in the rock, extending up very nearly to the cave above, which leads about twenty feet back to Louisa's Dome, a pretty little place of not more than twelve feet in diameter, but of twice that height. This dome is directly under the centre of the cave we had just been traversing, and when lighted up, persons within it can be plainly seen from above, through a crevice in the rock. Arrived at Gorin's Dome, we were forcibly struck by the seeming appearance of ***design***, in the arrangement of the several parts, for the special accommodation of visitors--even with reference to their number. The Labyrinth, which we followed up, brought us at its termination, to a window or hole, about four feet square, three feet above the floor, opening into the interior of the dome, about midway between the bottom and top; the wall of rock being at this spot, not more than eighteen inches thick; and continuing around, and on the outside of the dome, along a gallery of a few feet in width, for twenty or more paces, we arrived at another opening of much larger size, eligibly disposed, and commanding, like the first, a view of very nearly the whole interior space. Whilst we are arranging ourselves, the guide steals away, passes down, down, one knows not how, and is presently seen by the dim light of his lamp, fifty feet below, standing near the wall on the inside of the dome. The dome is of solid rock, with sides apparently fluted and polished, and perhaps two hundred feet high. Immediately in front and about thirty feet from the window, a huge rock seems suspended from above and arranged in folds like a curtain. Here we are then, the guide fifty feet below us. Some of the party thrusting their heads and, in their anxiety to see, their bodies through the window into the vast and gloomy dome of two hundred feet in height. The window is not large enough to afford a view to all at once, they crowd one on the top of the other; the more cautious, and those who do not like to be squeezed, stand back; but still holding fast to the garments of their friends for fear they might in the ecstasy of their feelings, leap into the frightful abyss into which they are looking. Suddenly the guide ignites a ***Bengal light***. The vast dome is radiant with light. Above, as far as the eye can reach, are seen the shining sides of the fluted walls; below, the yawning gulf is rendered the more terrific, by the pallid light exposing to view its vast depth, the whole displaying a scene of sublimity and splendor, such as words have not power to describe. Returning, we ascended the ladder near Louisa's Dome, and continued on, having the Labyrinth on our right side until it terminates in the Bottomless Pit. This pit terminates also the range of the Deserted Chambers, and was considered the Ultima Thule of all explorers, until within the last few years, when Mr. Stephenson of Georgetown, Ky. and the intrepid guide, Stephen, conceived the idea of reaching the opposite side by throwing a ladder across the frightful chasm. This they accomplished, and on this ladder, extending across a chasm of twenty feet wide and near two hundred deep, did these daring explorers cross to the opposite side, and thus open the way to all those splendid discoveries, which have added so much to the value and renown of the Mammoth Cave. The Bottomless Pit is somewhat in the shape of a horse-shoe, having a tongue of land twenty seven feet long, running out into the middle of it. From the end of this point of land, a substantial bridge has been thrown across to the cave on the opposite side.

While standing on the bridge, the guide lets down a lighted paper into the deep abyss; it descends twisting and turning, lower and lower, and is soon lost in total darkness, leaving us to conjecture, as to what may be below. Crossing the bridge to the opposite cave, we find ourselves in the midst of rocks of the most gigantic size lying along the edge of the pit and on our left hand. Above the pit is a dome of great size, but which, from its position, few have seen. Proceeding along a narrow passage for some distance, we arrived at the point from which diverge two noted routes--the Winding Way and Pensico Avenue. Here we called a short halt; then wishing our newly formed acquintances a safe voyage over the "deep waters," we parted; they taking the left hand to the Winding Way and the rivers, and we the right to Pensico Avenue.

CHAPTER VII.

Pensico Avenue--Great Crossings--Pine Apple Bush--Angelica's Grotto--Winding Way--Fat Friend in Trouble--Relief Hall--Bacon Chamber--Bandit's Hall.

Pensico Avenue averages about fifty feet in width, with a height of about thirty feet; and is said to be two miles long. It unites in an eminent degree the truly beautiful with the sublime, and is highly interesting throughout its entire extent. For a quarter of a mile from the entrance, the roof is beautifully arched, about twelve feet high and sixty wide, and formerly was encrusted with rosettes and other formations, nearly all of which have been taken away or demolished, leaving this section of the Cave quite denuded. The walking here is excellent; a dozen persons might run abreast for a quarter of a mile to Bunyan's Way, a branch of the avenue, leading on to the river. At this point the avenue changes its features of beauty and regularity, for those of wild grandeur and sublimity, which it preserves to the end. The way, no longer smooth and level, is frequently interrupted and turned aside by huge rocks, which lie tumbled around, in all imaginable disorder. The roof now becomes very lofty and imposingly magnificent; its long, pointed or lancet arches, forcibly reminding you of the rich and gorgeous ceilings of the old Gothic Cathedrals, at the same time solemnly impressing you with the conviction that this is a "building not made with hands." No one, not dead to all the more refined sensibilities of our nature, but must exclaim, in beholding the sublime scenes which here present themselves, this is not the work of man! No one can be here without being reminded of the all pervading presence of the great "Father of all."

"What, but God, pervades, adjusts and agitates the whole!"

Not far from the point at which the avenue assumes the rugged features, which now characterize it, we separated from our guide, he continuing his straight-forward course, and we descending gradually a few feet and entering a tunnel of fifteen feet wide on our left, the ceiling twelve or fourteen feet high, perfectly arched and beautifully covered with white incrustations, very soon reached the Great Crossings. Here the guide jumped down some six or eight feet from the avenue which we had left, into the tunnel where we were standing, and crossing it, climbed up into the avenue, which he pursued for a short distance or until it united with the tunnel, where he again joined us. In separating from, then crossing, and again uniting with the avenue, it describes with it something like the figure 8. The name, Great Crossings, is not unapt. It was however, not given, as our intelligent guide veritably assured us, in honor of the Great Crossings where the man lives who killed Tecumseh, but because two great caves cross here; and moreover said he, "the valiant Colonel ought to change the name of his place, as no two places in a State should bear the same name, and this being the ***great*** place ought to have the preference."

Not very far from this point, we ascended a hill on our left, and walking a short distance over our shoe-tops in dry nitrous earth, in a direction somewhat at a right angle with the avenue below, we arrived at the Pine Apple Bush, a large column, composed of a white, soft, crumbling material, with bifurcations extending from the floor to the ceiling. At a short distance, either to the right or left, you have a fine view of the avenue some twenty feet below, both up and down. Why this crumbling stalactite is called the Pine Apple Bush, I cannot divine. It stands however in a charming, secluded spot, inviting to repose; and we luxuriated in inhaling the all-inspiring air, while reclining on the clean, soft and dry salt petre earth.

All lovers of romantic scenery ought to visit this avenue, and all dyspeptic hypochondriacs and love-sick despondents should do likewise, for there is something wonderfully exhilarating in the air of Pensico. Our friend B. remarked while rolling on the salt petre earth at the Pine Apple Bush, that he felt "especially happy," and whether from sympathy, air or what not, we all partook of the same feeling. The guide seeing the position of our fat friend, and hearing his remark, said, laughing most immoderately, "these sort of feelings would come over one, now and then in the Cave, but wait till you get in the Winding Way and see how you feel then."

Having descended into the avenue we had left, we passed a number of stalactites and stalagmites, bearing a remarkable resemblance to coral, and a hundred or more paces beyond, arrived at a recess on the left, lined with innumerable crystals of dog-tooth spar, shining most brilliantly, called Angelica's Grotto. One would think it almost sacrilege to deface a spot like this; yet, did a Clergyman (the back of the guide being turned,) deliberately demolish a number of beautiful crystals to inscribe the initials of his name.

Returning to the head of Pensico Avenue, we turned to our right, and entered the narrow pass which leads to the river, pursuing which, for a few hundred yards, descending all the while, at one or two places down a ladder or stone steps, we came to a path cut through a high and broad embankment of sand, which very soon conducted us to the much talked of and anxiously looked for Winding Way. The Winding Way, has, in the opinion of many, been channeled in the rock by the gradual attrition of water. If this be so, and appearances seem to support such belief, at what early age of the world did the work commence? Was it not when "the earth was without form and void," thousands of years perhaps, before the date of the Mosaic account of the Creation? The Winding Way is one hundred and five feet long, eighteen inches wide, and from three to seven feet deep, widening out above, sufficiently to admit the free use of one's arms. It is throughout tortuous, a perfect *zig-zag*, the terror of the Falstaffs and the ladies of "fat, fair and forty," who have an instinctive dread of the trials to come, and are well aware of the merriment that their efforts to ***force a passage*** will excite among their companions of less length of girdle. Into this winding way, we entered in Indian file, and turning our right side, then our left, twisting this way, then that, had nearly made good the passage, when our ***fat friend***, who was puffing and blowing behind us like a high pressure engine, cried out, "Halt, ahead there! I am stuck as tight as a wedge in a log!" Halt we did, when the guide, looking at our friend, who was in truth "wedg'd in the rocky way and sticking fast," cried out, "I told you, when you said at the Pine Apple Bush, that you felt ***especially happy***, to wait till you got to the Winding Way, to see how you would feel then!" The imprisoned gentleman soon burst his bonds, not, however, without damage to his indispensables; and at length forcing his way into Relief Hall, he cried out, in the joy of his heart, while stretching himself and wiping the perspiration from his jolly, rubicund face, "never was a name more appropriate given to any place--Relief. I feel already the ***expansive faculty*** of the atmosphere,

I can now breathe again."

Relief Hall, which you enter from the Winding Way, at a right-angle, is very wide and lofty but not long; turning to the right, we reached its termination at River Hall, a distance of perhaps, one hundred yards. Here two routes present themselves; the one to the left conducts to the Dead Sea and the Rivers, and that to the right, to the Bacon Chamber, the Bandit's Hall, the Mammoth Dome and an infinity of other caves, domes, etc. We will speak of the Bacon Chamber; but before doing so, let us take our lunch. The air or exercise, or probably both, acted as powerful appetizers, and we soon gave proof that we needed not Stoughton's bitters to provoke an appetite. Having discussed a few glasses of excellent Hock, we left the Bacon Chamber, which is a pretty fair representation of a low ceiling, thickly hung with canvassed hams and shoulders; and proceeded to the Bandit's Hall, up a steep ascent of twenty or thirty feet, rendered very difficult, by the huge rocks which obstructed the way and over which we were forced to clamber. The name is indicative of the spot. It is a vast and lofty chamber, the floor covered with a mountainous heap of rocks rising amphitheatrically almost to the ceiling, and so disposed as to furnish at different elevations, galleries or platforms, reaching immediately around the chamber itself or leading off into some of its hidden recesses. The guide is presently seen standing at a fearful height above, and suddenly a Bengal light, blazes up, "when the rugged roof, the frowning cliffs and the whole chaos of rocks are refulgent in the brilliant glare." The sublimity of the scene is beyond the powers of the imagination.

CHAPTER VIII.

Mammoth Dome--First Discoverers--Little Dome--Tale of a Lamp--Return.

From the Bandit's Hall, diverge two caves; one of which, the left, leads you to a multitude of domes; and the right, to one which, *par excellence*, is called the Mammoth Dome. Taking the right, we arrived, after a rugged walk of nearly a mile, to a platform, which commands an indistinct view of this dome of domes. It was discovered by a German gentleman and the guide Stephen about two years ago, but was not explored until some months after, when it was visited by a party of four or five, accompanied by two guides, and well prepared with ropes, &c. From the platform, the guides were let down about twenty feet, by means of a rope, and upon reaching the ground below, they found themselves on the side of a hill, which, descending about fifty feet, brought them immediately under the Great Dome, from the summit of which, there is a water-fall. This dome is near four hundred feet high, and is justly considered one of the most sublime and wonderful spectacles of this most wonderful of caverns. From the bottom of the dome they ascended the hill to the place to which they had been lowered from the platform, and continuing thence up a very steep hill, more than one hundred feet, they reached its summit. Arrived at the summit, a scene of awful grandeur and magnificence is presented to the view. Looking down the declivity, you see far below to the left, the visiters whom you have left behind, standing on the platform or termination of the avenue along which they had come; and lower down still, the bottom of the Great Dome itself. Above, two hundred and eighty feet, is the ceiling, lost in the obscurity of space and distance. The height of the ceiling was determined by E.F. Lee, civil engineer. This fact in regard to the elevation of the ceiling and the locality of the Great Hall, was subsequently ascertained, by finding on the summit of the hill, (a spot never before trodden by man,) an iron lamp!! The astonishment of the guides, as well as of the whole party, on beholding the lamp, can be easily imagined; and to this day they would have been ignorant of its history, but for the accidental circumstance of an old man being at the Cave Hotel, who, thirty years ago, was engaged as a miner in the saltpetre establishment of Wilkins & Gratz. He, on being shown the lamp, said at once, that it had been found under the crevice pit (a fact that surprised all,); that during the time Wilkins & Gratz were engaged in the manufacture of saltpetre, a Mr. Gatewood informed Wilkins, that in all probability, the richest nitre earth was under the crevice pit. The depth of this pit being then unknown, Wilkins, to ascertain it, got a rope of 45 feet long, and fastening this identical lamp to the end of it, lowered it into the pit, in the doing of which, the string caught on fire, and down fell the lamp. Wilkins made an offer of two dollars to any one of the miners who would descend the pit and bring up the lamp. His offer was accepted by a man, who, in consequence of his diminutive stature, was nicknamed Little Dave; and the rope being made fast about his waist, he, torch in hand, was lowered to the full extent of the forty-five feet. Being then drawn up, the poor fellow was found to be so excessively alarmed, that he could scarcely articulate; but having recovered from his fright, and again with the full power of utterance, he declared that no money could tempt him to try again for the lamp; and in excuse for such a determination, he related the most marvellous story of what he had seen--far exceeding the wonderful things which the unexampled Don Quixote de la Mancha declared he had seen in the deep cave of Montesinos. Dave was, in fact, suspended at the height of two hundred and forty feet above the level below. Such is the history of the *lamp*, as told by the old miner, Holton, the correctness of which was very soon verified; for guides having been sent to the place where the lamp was found, and persons at the same time stationed at the mouth of the crevice pit, their proximity was at once made manifest by the very audible sound of each other's voices, and by the fact that sticks thrown into the pit fell at the feet of the guides below, and were brought out by them. The distance from the mouth of the Cave to this pit, falls short of half a mile; yet to reach the grand apartment immediately under it, requires a circuit to be made of at least three miles. The illumination of that portion of the Great Dome on the left, and of the hall on the top of the hill to the right, as seen from the platform, was unquestionably one of the most impressive spectacles we had witnessed; but to be seen to advantage, another position ought to be taken by the spectator, and the dome with its towering height, and the hall on the summit of the hill, with its gigantic stalagmite columns, and ceiling two hundred feet high, illuminated by the simultaneous ignition of a number of Bengal lights, judiciously arranged. Such was the enthusiastic admiration of some foreigners on witnessing an illumination of the Great Dome and Hall, that they declared, it alone would compensate for a voyage across the Atlantic. With the partial illumination of the Great Dome, we closed our explorations on this side of the rivers, and retracing our steps, reached the hotel about sun-set. At mid-night, the party which separated from us at the entrance of Pensico Avenue, returned from the points beyond the Echo river.

CHAPTER IX.

Third Visit--River Hall--Dead Sea--River Styx--Lethe--Echo River-- Purgatory--Eyeless Fish--Supposed Boil of the Rivers--Sources and Outlet Unknown.

Early the next morning, having made all the necessary preparations for the grand tour, which we were the more anxious to take from the glowing accounts of the party recently returned, we entered the cave immediately after an early breakfast, and proceeded rapidly on to River Hall. It was evident from the appearance of the flood here, that it had been recently overflown.

"The cave, or the River Hall," remarks a fair and distinguished authoress, whose description of the river scenery is so graphic, that I cannot do better than transcribe it throughout: "The River Hall descends like the slope of a mountain; the ceiling stretches away--away before you, vast and grand as the firmament at midnight." Going on, and gradually ascending and keeping close to the right hand wall, you observe on your left "a steep precipice, over which you can look down by the aid of blazing missiles, upon a broad black sheet of water, eighty feet below, called the Dead Sea. This is an awfully impressive place; the sights and sounds of which, do not easily pass from memory. He who has seen it, will have it vividly brought before him, by Alfieri's description of Filippo, 'only a transient word or act gives us a short and dubious glimmer, that reveals to us the abysses of his being--dark, lurid and terrific, as the throat of the infernal pool.' Descending from the eminence, by a ladder of about twenty feet, we find ourselves among piles of gigantic rocks, and one of the most picturesque sights in the world, is to see a file of men and women passing along those wild and scraggy paths, moving slowly--slowly, that their lamps may have time to illuminate their sky-like ceiling and gigantic walls--disappearing behind high cliffs--sinking into ravines--their lights shining upwards through fissures in the rocks--then suddenly emerging from some abrupt angle, standing in the bright gleam of their lamps, relieved by the towering black masses around them. He, who could paint the infinite variety of creation, can alone give an adequate idea of this marvellous region. As you pass along, you hear the roar of invisible waterfalls; and at the foot of the slope, the river Styx lies before you, deep and black, overarched with rock. The first glimpse of it brings to mind, the descent of Ulysses into hell,

"Where the dark rock o'erhangs the infernal lake,
And mingling streams eternal murmurs make."

Across (or rather down) these unearthly waters, the guide can convey but four passengers at once. The lamps are fastened to the prow; the images of which, are reflected in the dismal pool. If you are impatient of delay, or eager for new adventures, you can leave your companions lingering about the shore, and cross the Styx by a dangerous bridge of precipices overhead. In order to do this, you must ascend a steep cliff, and enter a cave above, 300 yards long, from an egress of which, you find yourself on the bank of the river, eighty feet above its surface, commanding a view of those in the boat, and those waiting on the shore. Seen from this height, the lamps in the canoe glare like fiery eye-balls; and the passengers, sitting there so hushed and motionless, look like shadows. The scene is so strangely funereal and spectral, that it seems as if the Greeks must have witnessed it, before they imagined Charon conveying ghosts to the dim regions of Pluto. Your companions thus seen, do indeed--

"Skim along the dusky glades,   Thin airy souls, and visionary shades."

If you turn your eyes from the canoe to the parties of men and women whom you left waiting on the shore, you will see them by the gleam of their lamps, scattered in picturesque groups, looming out in bold relief from the dense darkness around them.

Having passed the Styx, (much the smallest of the rivers,) you walk over a pile of large rocks, and are on the banks of Lethe; and looking back, you will see a line of men and women descending the high hill from the cave, which runs **over** the river Styx. Here are two boats, and the parties, which have come by the two routes, **down** the Styx or **over** it, uniting, descend the Lethe about a quarter of a mile, the ceiling for the entire distance being very high--certainly not less than fifty feet. On landing, you enter a level and lofty hall, called the Great Walk, which stretches to the banks of the Echo, a distance of three or four hundred yards. The Echo is truly a river: it is wide and deep enough, at all times, to float the largest steamer. At the point of embarkation, the arch is very low, not more than three feet, in an ordinary stage of water, being left for a boat to pass through. Passengers, of course, are obliged to double up, and lie upon each others shoulders, in a most uncomfortable way, but their suffering is of short duration; in two boat lengths, they emerge to where the vault of the cave is lofty and wide. The boat in which we embarked was sufficiently large to carry twelve persons, and our voyage down the river was one of deep, indeed of most intense interest. The novelty, the grandeur, the magnificence of every thing around elicited unbounded admiration and wonder. All sense of danger, (had any been experienced before,) was lost in the solemn, quiet sublimity of the scene. The rippling of the water caused by the motion of our boat is heard afar off, beating under the low arches and in the cavities of the rocks. The report of a pistol is as that of the heaviest artillery, and long and afar does the echo resound, like the muttering of distant thunder. The voice of song was raised on this dark, deep water, and the sound was as that of the most powerful choir. A full band of music on this river of echoes would indeed be overpowering. The aquatic excursion was more to our taste than any thing we had seen, and never can the impression it made be obliterated from our memories.

The Echo is three quarters of a mile long. A rise of the water of merely a few feet connects the three rivers. After long and heavy rains, these rivers sometimes rise to a perpendicular height of more than fifty feet; and then they, as well as the cataracts, exhibit a most terrific appearance. The low arch at the entrance of the Echo, can not be passed when there is a rise of water of even two feet. Once or twice parties have been caught on the further side by a sudden rise, and for a time their alarm was great, not knowing that there was an upper cave through which they could pass, that would lead them around the arch to the Great Walk. This upper cave, or passage, is called Purgatory, and is, for a distance of forty feet, so low, that persons have to crawl on their faces, or, as the guides say, **snake it**. We were pleased to learn that this passage would soon be sufficiently enlarged to enable persons to walk through erect. This accomplished, an excursion to Cleveland's Avenue may be made almost entirely by land, at the same time that all apprehensions of being caught beyond Echo will be removed. It is in these rivers, that the extraordinary white eyeless fish are caught--we secured two of them. There is not the slightest indication of an organ similar to an eye, to be discovered. They have been dissected by skillful anatomists, who declare that they are not only without eyes, but also develope other anomalies in their organization, singularly interesting to the naturalist. "The rivers of Mammoth Cave were never crossed till 1840. Great efforts have been made to discover whence they come and whither they go, yet they still remain as much a mystery as ever--without beginning or end; like eternity."

"Darkly thou glidest onward,
Thou deep and hidden wave!
The laughing sunshine hath not look'd
Into thy secret cave.

Thy current makes no music--
A hollow sound we hear;
A muffled voice of mystery,
And know that thou art near.

No brighter line of verdure
Follows thy lonely way
No fairy moss, or lily's cup,
Is freshened by thy play."

According to the barometrical measurement of Professor Locke, the rivers of the Cave are nearly on a level with Green River; but the report of Mr. Lee, civil engineer, is widely different. He says, "The bottom of the Little Bat Room Pit is one hundred and twenty feet **below** the bed of Green River. The Bottomless Pit is also deeper than the bed of Green River, and so far as a surveyor's level can be relied on, the same may be said of the Cavern Pit and some others." The rivers of the Cave were unknown at the time of Mr. Lee's visit in 1835, but they are unquestionably ***lower*** than the bottom of the pits, and receive the water which flows from them. According to the statement of Lee, the bed of these rivers is lower than the bed of Green River at its junction with the Ohio, taking for granted that the report of the State engineers as to the extent of fall between a point above the Cave and the Ohio, be correct, of which there is no doubt. "It becomes, then," continues Mr. Lee, in reference to the waters of the Cave, "an object of interesting inquiry to determine in what way it is disposed of. If it empties into Green River, the Ohio, or the ocean, it must run a great distance under ground, with a very small descent."

CHAPTER X.

Pass of El Ghor--Silliman's Avenue--Wellington's Gallery--Sulphur Spring--Mary's Vineyard--Holy Sepulchre--Commencement of Cleveland Avenue--By whom Discovered--Beautiful Formations--Snow-ball Room--Rocky Mountains--Croghan's Hall--Serena's Arbor--Dining Table--Dinner Party and Toast--Hoax of the Guide--Homeward Bound Passage--Conclusion.

Having now left the Echo, we have a walk of four miles to Cleveland's Avenue. The intervening points are of great interest; but it would occupy too much time to describe them. We will therefore hurry on through the pass of El Ghor, Silliman's Avenue, and Wellington's Gallery, to the foot of the ladder which leads up to the Elysium of Mammoth cave. And here, for the benefit of the weary and thirsty, and of all others whom it may interest, coming after us, be it known, that Carneal's Spring is close at hand, and equally near, a sulphur spring, the water of which, equals in quality and quantity that of the farfamed White Sulphur Spring, of Virginia. At the head of the ladder, you find yourself surrounded by overhanging stalactites, in the form of rich clusters of grapes, hard as flint, and round and polished, as if done by a sculptor's hand. This is called Mary's Vineyard--the commencement of Cleveland's Avenue, the crowning wonder and glory of this subterranean world. Proceeding to the right about, a hundred feet from this spot, over a rough and rather difficult way, you reach the base of the height or hill, on which, stands the Holy Sepulchre. This interesting spot is reached at some hazard, as the ascent, which is very steep, and more than twenty feet high, affords no secure footing, owing to the loose and shingly character of the surface, until the height is gained. Having achieved this, you stand immediately at the beautiful door-way of the Chapel, or anteroom of the Sepulchre. This Chapel, which is, perhaps, twelve feet square, with a low ceiling, and decorated in the most gorgeous manner, with well-arranged draperies of stalactite of every imaginable shape, leads you to the room of the Holy Sepulchre adjoining, which is without ornament or decoration of any kind; exhibiting nothing but dark and bare walls--like a charnel house. In the centre of this room, which stands a few feet below the Chapel, is, to all appearance, a grave, hewn out of the living rock. This is the Holy Sepulchre. A Roman Catholic priest discovered it about three years ago, and with fervent enthusiasm exclaimed, "The Holy Sepulchre!" a name which it has since borne. Returning from the Holy Sepulchre, we commence our wanderings through Cleveland's Avenue--an avenue three miles long, seventy feet wide, and twelve or fifteen feet high--an avenue more rich and gorgeous than any ever revealed to man--an avenue abounding in formations such as are no where else to be seen, and which the most stupid observer could not behold without feelings of wonder and admiration. Some of the formations in the avenue, have been denominated by Professor Locke, oulophilites, or curled leafed stone; and in remarking upon them, he says, "They are unlike any thing yet discovered; equally beautiful for the cabinet of the amateur, and interesting to the geological philosopher." And I, although a wanderer myself in various climes, and somewhat of a mineralogist withal, have never seen or heard of such. Apprehensive that I might, in attempting to describe much that I have seen, color too highly, I will, in lieu thereof, offer the remarks of an intelligent clergyman, extracted from the New York Christian Observer, of a recent date: "The most imaginative poet never conceived or painted a palace of such exquisite beauty and loveliness, as Cleveland's Cabinet, into which you now pass. Were the wealth of princes bestowed on the most skilful lapidaries, with the view of rivaling the splendors of this single chamber, the attempt would be vain. How then can I hope to give you a conception of it? You must see it; and you will then feel that all attempt at description, is futile." The Cabinet was discovered by Mr. Patten, of Louisville, and Mr. Craig, of Philadelphia, accompanied by the guide Stephen, and extends in nearly a direct line about one and a half miles, (the guides say two miles.) It is a perfect arch, of fifty feet span, and of an average height of ten feet in the centre--just high enough to be viewed with ease in all its parts. It is incrusted from end to end with the most beautiful formations, in every variety of form. The base of the whole, is carbonate (sulphate) of lime, in part of dazzling whiteness, and perfectly smooth, and in other places crystallized so as to glitter like diamonds in the light. Growing from this, in endlessly diversified forms, is a substance resembling selenite, translucent and imperfectly laminated. It is most probably sulphate of lime, (a gypsum,) combined with sulphate of magnesia. Some of the crystals bear a striking resemblance to branches of celery, and all about the same length; while others, a foot or more in length, have the color and appearance of **vanilla cream candy**; others are set in sulphate of lime, in the form of a rose; and others still roll out from the base, in forms resembling the ornaments on the capitol of a Corinthian column. (You see how I am driven for analogies.) Some of the incrustations are massive and splendid; others are as delicate as the lily, or as fancy-work of shell or wax. Think of traversing an arched way like this for a mile and a half, and all the wonders of the tales of youth--"Arabian Nights," and all--seem tame, compared with the living, growing reality. Yes, **growing** reality; for the process is going on before your eyes. Successive coats of these incrustations, have been perfected and crowded off by others; so that hundreds of tons of these gems lie at your feet, and are crushed as you pass, while the work of restoring the ornaments for nature's **boudoir**, is proceeding around you. Here and there, through the whole extent, you will find openings in the sides, into which you may thrust the person, and often stand erect in little grottoes, perfectly incrusted with a delicate white substance, reflecting the light from a thousand glittering points. All the way you might have heard us exclaiming, "Wonderful, wonderful! O, Lord, how manifold are thy works!" With general unity of form and appearance, there is considerable variety in "the Cabinet." The "**Snow-ball Room**," for example, is a section of the cave described above, some 200 feet in length, entirely different from the adjacent parts; its appearance being aptly indicated by its name. If a hundred rude school boys had but an hour before completed their day's sport, by throwing a thousand snow-balls against the roof, while an equal number were scattered about the floor, and all petrified, it would have presented precisely such a scene as you witness in this room of nature's frolics. So far as I know, these "snow-balls" are a perfect anomaly among all the strange forms of crystalization. It is the result, I presume, of an unusual combination of the sulphates of lime and magnesia, with a carbonate of the former. We found here and elsewhere in the Cabinet, fine specimens of the sulphate of Magnesia, (or Epsom salts,) a foot or two long, and three inches in thickness.

Leaving the quiet and beautiful "Cabinet," you come suddenly upon the "Rocky Mountains," furnishing a contrast so bold and striking, as almost to startle you. Clambering up the rough side some thirty feet, you pass close under the roof of the cavern you have left, and find before you an immense transverse cave, 100 feet or more from the ceiling to the floor, with a huge pile of rocks half filling the hither side--they were probably dashed from the roof in the great earthquake of 1811. Taking the left hand branch, you are soon brought to "Croghan's Hall," which is nine miles from the mouth, and is the farthest point explored in that direction. The "Hall" is 50 or 60 feet in diameter, and perhaps, thirty-five feet high, of a semi-circular form. Fronting you as you enter, are massive stalactites, ten or fifteen feet in length, attached to the rock, like sheets of ice, and of a brilliant color. The rock projects near the floor, and then recedes with a regular and graceful curve, or swell, leaving a cavity of several feet in width between it and the floor. At intervals, around this swell, stalactites of various forms are suspended, and behind the sheet of stalactites first described, are numerous stalagmites, in fanciful forms. I brought one away that resembles the horns of the deer, being nearly translucent. In the centre of this hall, a very large stalactite hangs from the roof; and a corresponding stalagmite rises from the floor, about three feet in height and a foot in diameter, of an amber color, perfectly smooth and translucent, like the other formations. On the right, is a deep pit, down which the water dashes from a cascade that pours from the roof. Other avenues could most likely be found by sounding the sides of the pit, if any one had the courage to attempt the descent. We are far enough from **terra supra**, and our dinner which we had left at the "Vineyard." We hastened back to the Rocky Mountains, and took the branch which we left at our right on emerging from the Cabinet. Pursuing the uneven path for some distance, we reached "Serena's Arbor," which was discovered but three months since, by our guide "Mat." The descent to the Arbor seemed so perilous, from the position of the loose rocks around, that several of the party would not venture. Those of us who scrambled down regarded this as the crowning object of interest. The "Arbor" is not more than twelve feet in diameter, and of about the same height, of a circular form; but is, of itself, floor, sides, roof, and ornaments, one perfect, seamless stalactite, of a beautiful hue, and exquisite workmanship. Folds or blades of stalactitic matter hang like drapery around the sides, reaching half way to the floor; and opposite the door, a canopy of stone projects, elegantly ornamented, as if it were the resting-place of a fairy bride. Every thing seemed fresh and new; indeed, the invisible architect has not quite finished this master-piece; for you can see the pure water, trickling down its tiny channels and perfecting the delicate points of some of the stalactites. Victoria, with all her splendor, has not in Windsor Castle, so beautiful an apartment as "Serena's Arbor."

Such is the description of Cleveland's Avenue, as given by this clerical gentleman. It is perfectly graphic, and corresponds with all the glowing accounts I have read of this famous place. Exquisitely beautiful and rare as are the formations in this avenue, it will soon be, I fear, like the Grotto of Pensico--shorn of its beauties. Many a little Miss, to decorate her centre table or boudoir, and many a thoughtless dandy to present a specimen to his lady fair, have broken from the walls (regardless of the published rules prohibiting it,) those lovely productions of the Almighty, which required ages to perfect; thus destroying in a moment the work of centuries. These beautiful and gorgeous formations were encrusted on the walls by the hands of our Maker, and who so impious as to desecrate them--to tear them from their place? there they are, all lovely and beautiful, and there they ought to remain, **_untouched_** by the hands of man, for the admiration and wonder of all future ages. If the comparatively small cave of Adelburg which belongs to the Emperor of Austria, be placed for the preservation of its formations under the protecting care of the government (as is the case,) what ought not to be done to preserve the mineralogical treasures, in this great Cave of America, and especially in Cleveland's Cabinet, which are worth more than all the caves in Europe, indeed of the world, so far as our knowledge of caverns extends.

Returning from Serena's Arbor, we passed on our left the mouth of an avenue more than three miles long, lofty and wide, and at its termination there is a hall, which in the opinion of the guide is larger than any other in the Cave. It is as yet without a name. Equidistant from the commencement and the termination of Cleveland's Avenue, is a huge rock, nearly circular, flat on the top and three feet high. This is the "**_dining table_**." More than one hundred persons could be seated around this table; on it the guide arranged our dinner, and we luxuriated on "flesh and fowl" and "choice old sherry." Never did a set of fellows enjoy dinner more than we did ours. Our friend B. was perfectly at his ease and happy; and, in the exuberance of his spirits, proposed the following toast:

> "Prosperity to the subterranean territory of Cimmeria; large enough, if not populous enough, for admission into the Union as an independent State."

We emptied our glasses and gave nine hearty cheers in honor of the sentiment. A proposition was made to adjourn, but B. was not inclined to locomotion, and opposed it with great warmth, insisting that it was too soon to move after such a dinner, and that a state of rest was absolutely essential to healthy digestion. We had much argument on the motion to adjourn; when our sagacious guide Stephen, with a meaning look interposed, saying "we had as well be going, for the river might take a rise and shut us up here." "What!" exclaimed B. in utter consternation, and with a start, literally bouncing from his seat, cried aloud "Let's be off!" at the same time suiting the action to the word. In a second we were all in motion, and hurrying past beautiful incrustations, through galleries long and tortuous, down one hill and up another, (poor B. puffing and blowing, and all the while exclaiming against the ***terrible*** length and ruggedness of the way,) we at last reached the Echo, which we found to our great relief had ***not risen***. It seems, the guide had used this stratagem for our own advantage, to break off our banquet, lest it trenched too far upon the night. We were too happy in having our fears relieved, to fall out with him. On our homeward bound passage over the rivers, our admiration was rather increased than diminished. The death-like stillness! the awful silence! the wild grandeur and sublimity of the scene, tranquilizing the feeling and disposing to pensive musings and quiet contemplation; on a sudden a pistol is fired--a tremendous report ensues--its echoes are heard reverberating from wall to wall, in caves far away, like the low murmuring sound of distant thunder--the spell of silence and deep reverie is broken--we become roused and animated, and the mighty cavern resounds with our song. We believe every one will, under similar circumstances, experience this sudden transition from pensive musings to joyous hilarity. Leaving the rivers, we hastened onward to the outlet to the upper world. Far ahead we perceive the first ***dawnings of day***, shining with a silvery pallid hue on the walls, and increasing in brightness as we advance, until it bursts forth in all the golden rays and glorious effulgence of the setting sun. This ***parting*** scene is lovely and interesting. We bid adieu to the "Great Monarch of Caves." We here terminate our subterranean tour. Standing on the grassy terrace above, we inhale the cool, pure air, and take a last look at the "great Wonder of Wonders!" To all we would say "go and see--explore the greatest of the Almighty's subterranean works." No description can give you an idea of it--neither can inspection of other caves; it is "the Monarch of Caves!" none that have ever been measured can at all compare with it, in extent, in grandeur, in wild, solemn, serene, unadorned majesty; it stands entirely alone.--"It has no brother; it has no brother."

www.bookjungle.com email: sales@bookjungle.com fax: 630-214-0564 mail: Book Jungle PO Box 2226 Champaign, IL 61825

The Codes Of Hammurabi And Moses
W. W. Davies

The discovery of the Hammurabi Code is one of the greatest achievements of archaeology, and is of paramount interest, not only to the student of the Bible, but also to all those interested in ancient history...

Religion   **ISBN:** *1-59462-338-4*   Pages:132   MSRP *$12.95*   QTY

The Theory of Moral Sentiments
Adam Smith

This work from 1749. contains original theories of conscience amd moral judgment and it is the foundation for systemof morals.

Philosophy   **ISBN:** *1-59462-777-0*   Pages:536   MSRP *$19.95*   QTY

Jessica's First Prayer
Hesba Stretton

In a screened and secluded corner of one of the many railway-bridges which span the streets of London there could be seen a few years ago, from five o'clock every morning until half past eight, a tidily set-out coffee-stall, consisting of a trestle and board, upon which stood two large tin cans, with a small fire of charcoal burning under each so as to keep the coffee boiling during the early hours of the morning when the work-people were thronging into the city on their way to their daily toil...

Childrens   **ISBN:** *1-59462-373-2*   Pages:84   MSRP *$9.95*   QTY

My Life and Work
Henry Ford

Henry Ford revolutionized the world with his implementation of mass production for the Model T automobile. Gain valuable business insight into his life and work with his own auto-biography... "We have only started on our development of our country we have not as yet, with all our talk of wonderful progress, done more than scratch the surface. The progress has been wonderful enough but..."

Biographies/   **ISBN:** *1-59462-198-5*   Pages:300   MSRP *$21.95*   QTY

www.bookjungle.com *email: sales@bookjungle.com fax: 630-214-0564 mail: Book Jungle PO Box 2226 Champaign, IL 61825*

The Art of Cross-Examination
Francis Wellman

QTY

I presume it is the experience of every author, after his first book is published upon an important subject, to be almost overwhelmed with a wealth of ideas and illustrations which could readily have been included in his book, and which to his own mind, at least, seem to make a second edition inevitable. Such certainly was the case with me; and when the first edition had reached its sixth impression in five months, I rejoiced to learn that it seemed to my publishers that the book had met with a sufficiently favorable reception to justify a second and considerably enlarged edition. ..

Reference   ISBN: *1-59462-647-2*   Pages:412   MSRP *$19.95*

On the Duty of Civil Disobedience
Henry David Thoreau

QTY

Thoreau wrote his famous essay, On the Duty of Civil Disobedience, as a protest against an unjust but popular war and the immoral but popular institution of slave-owning. He did more than write—he declined to pay his taxes, and was hauled off to gaol in consequence. Who can say how much this refusal of his hastened the end of the war and of slavery ?

Law   ISBN: *1-59462-747-9*   Pages:48   MSRP *$7.45*

Dream Psychology Psychoanalysis for Beginners
Sigmund Freud

QTY

Sigmund Freud, born Sigismund Schlomo Freud (May 6, 1856 - September 23, 1939), was a Jewish-Austrian neurologist and psychiatrist who co-founded the psychoanalytic school of psychology. Freud is best known for his theories of the unconscious mind, especially involving the mechanism of repression; his redefinition of sexual desire as mobile and directed towards a wide variety of objects; and his therapeutic techniques, especially his understanding of transference in the therapeutic relationship and the presumed value of dreams as sources of insight into unconscious desires.

Psychology   ISBN: *1-59462-905-6*   Pages:196   MSRP *$15.45*

The Miracle of Right Thought
Orison Swett Marden

QTY

Believe with all of your heart that you will do what you were made to do. When the mind has once formed the habit of holding cheerful, happy, prosperous pictures, it will not be easy to form the opposite habit. It does not matter how improbable or how far away this realization may see, or how dark the prospects may be, if we visualize them as best we can, as vividly as possible, hold tenaciously to them and vigorously struggle to attain them, they will gradually become actualized, realized in the life. But a desire, a longing without endeavor, a yearning abandoned or held indifferently will vanish without realization.

Self Help   ISBN: *1-59462-644-8*   Pages:360   MSRP *$25.45*

www.bookjungle.com email: sales@bookjungle.com fax: 630-214-0564 mail: Book Jungle PO Box 2226 Champaign, IL 61825

QTY

	Title	ISBN	Price
☐	**The Rosicrucian Cosmo-Conception Mystic Christianity** by *Max Heindel*	ISBN: 1-59462-188-8	$38.95
	The Rosicrucian Cosmo-conception is not dogmatic, neither does it appeal to any other authority than the reason of the student. It is: not controversial, but is: sent forth in the, hope that it may help to clear...	New Age/Religion Pages 646	
☐	**Abandonment To Divine Providence** by *Jean-Pierre de Caussade*	ISBN: 1-59462-228-0	$25.95
	"The Rev. Jean Pierre de Caussade was one of the most remarkable spiritual writers of the Society of Jesus in France in the 18th Century. His death took place at Toulouse in 1751. His works have gone through many editions and have been republished...	Inspirational/Religion Pages 400	
☐	**Mental Chemistry** by *Charles Haanel*	ISBN: 1-59462-192-6	$23.95
	Mental Chemistry allows the change of material conditions by combining and appropriately utilizing the power of the mind. Much like applied chemistry creates something new and unique out of careful combinations of chemicals the mastery of mental chemistry...	New Age Pages 354	
☐	**The Letters of Robert Browning and Elizabeth Barret Barrett 1845-1846 vol II** by Robert Browning and Elizabeth Barrett	ISBN: 1-59462-193-4	$35.95
		Biographies Pages 596	
☐	**Gleanings In Genesis (volume I)** by *Arthur W. Pink*	ISBN: 1-59462-130-6	$27.45
	Appropriately has Genesis been termed "the seed plot of the Bible" for in it we have, in germ form, almost all of the great doctrines which are afterwards fully developed in the books of Scripture which follow...	Religion/Inspirational Pages 420	
☐	**The Master Key** by *L. W. de Laurence*	ISBN: 1-59462-001-6	$30.95
	In no branch of human knowledge has there been a more lively increase of the spirit of research during the past few years than in the study of Psychology, Concentration and Mental Discipline. The requests for authentic lessons in Thought Control, Mental Discipline and...	New Age/Business Pages 422	
☐	**The Lesser Key Of Solomon Goetia** by *L. W. de Laurence*	ISBN: 1-59462-092-X	$9.95
	This translation of the first book of the "Lernegton" which is now for the first time made accessible to students of Talismanic Magic was done, after careful collation and edition, from numerous Ancient Manuscripts in Hebrew, Latin, and French...	New Age/Occult Pages 92	
☐	**Rubaiyat Of Omar Khayyam** by *Edward Fitzgerald*	ISBN:1-59462-332-5	$13.95
	Edward Fitzgerald, whom the world has already learned, in spite of his own efforts to remain within the shadow of anonymity, to look upon as one of the rarest poets of the century, was born at Bredfield, in Suffolk, on the 31st of March, 1809. He was the third son of John Purcell...	Music Pages 172	
☐	**Ancient Law** by *Henry Maine*	ISBN: 1-59462-128-4	$29.95
	The chief object of the following pages is to indicate some of the earliest ideas of mankind, as they are reflected in Ancient Law, and to point out the relation of those ideas to modern thought.	Religion/History Pages 452	
☐	**Far-Away Stories** by *William J. Locke*	ISBN: 1-59462-129-2	$19.45
	"Good wine needs no bush, but a collection of mixed vintages does. And this book is just such a collection. Some of the stories I do not want to remain buried for ever in the museum files of dead magazine-numbers an author's not unpardonable vanity..."	Fiction Pages 272	
☐	**Life of David Crockett** by *David Crockett*	ISBN: 1-59462-250-7	$27.45
	"Colonel David Crockett was one of the most remarkable men of the times in which he lived. Born in humble life, but gifted with a strong will, an indomitable courage, and unremitting perseverance...	Biographies/New Age Pages 424	
☐	**Lip-Reading** by *Edward Nitchie*	ISBN: 1-59462-206-X	$25.95
	Edward B. Nitchie, founder of the New York School for the Hard of Hearing, now the Nitchie School of Lip-Reading, Inc, wrote "LIP-READING Principles and Practice". The development and perfecting of this meritorious work on lip-reading was an undertaking...	How-to Pages 400	
☐	**A Handbook of Suggestive Therapeutics, Applied Hypnotism, Psychic Science** by *Henry Munro*	ISBN: 1-59462-214-0	$24.95
		Health/New Age/Health/Self-help Pages 376	
☐	**A Doll's House: and Two Other Plays** by *Henrik Ibsen*	ISBN: 1-59462-112-8	$19.95
	Henrik Ibsen created this classic when in revolutionary 1848 Rome. Introducing some striking concepts in playwriting for the realist genre, this play has been studied the world over.	Fiction/Classics/Plays 308	
☐	**The Light of Asia** by *sir Edwin Arnold*	ISBN: 1-59462-204-3	$13.95
	In this poetic masterpiece, Edwin Arnold describes the life and teachings of Buddha. The man who was to become known as Buddha to the world was born as Prince Gautama of India but he rejected the worldly riches and abandoned the reigns of power when...	Religion/History/Biographies Pages 170	
☐	**The Complete Works of Guy de Maupassant** by *Guy de Maupassant*	ISBN: 1-59462-157-8	$16.95
	"For days and days, nights and nights, I had dreamed of that first kiss which was to consecrate our engagement, and I knew not on what spot I should put my lips..."	Fiction/Classics Pages 240	
☐	**The Art of Cross-Examination** by *Francis L. Wellman*	ISBN: 1-59462-309-0	$26.95
	Written by a renowned trial lawyer, Wellman imparts his experience and uses case studies to explain how to use psychology to extract desired information through questioning.	How-to/Science/Reference Pages 408	
☐	**Answered or Unanswered?** by *Louisa Vaughan*	ISBN: 1-59462-248-5	$10.95
	Miracles of Faith in China	Religion Pages 112	
☐	**The Edinburgh Lectures on Mental Science (1909)** by *Thomas*	ISBN: 1-59462-008-3	$11.95
	This book contains the substance of a course of lectures recently given by the writer in the Queen Street Hall, Edinburgh. Its purpose is to indicate the Natural Principles governing the relation between Mental Action and Material Conditions...	New Age/Psychology Pages 148	
☐	**Ayesha** by *H. Rider Haggard*	ISBN: 1-59462-301-5	$24.95
	Verily and indeed it is the unexpected that happens! Probably if there was one person upon the earth from whom the Editor of this, and of a certain previous history, did not expect to hear again...	Classics Pages 380	
☐	**Ayala's Angel** by *Anthony Trollope*	ISBN: 1-59462-352-X	$29.95
	The two girls were both pretty, but Lucy who was twenty-one who supposed to be simple and comparatively unattractive, whereas Ayala was credited, as her Bombwhat romantic name might show, with poetic charm and a taste for romance. Ayala when her father died was nineteen...	Fiction Pages 484	
☐	**The American Commonwealth** by *James Bryce*	ISBN: 1-59462-286-8	$34.45
	An interpretation of American democratic political theory. It examines political mechanics and society from the perspective of Scotsman James Bryce	Politics Pages 572	
☐	**Stories of the Pilgrims** by *Margaret P. Pumphrey*	ISBN: 1-59462-116-0	$17.95
	This book explores pilgrims religious oppression in England as well as their escape to Holland and eventual crossing to America on the Mayflower, and their early days in New England...	History Pages 268	

www.bookjungle.com email: sales@bookjungle.com fax: 630-214-0564 mail: Book Jungle PO Box 2226 Champaign, IL 61825

QTY

The Fasting Cure *by Sinclair Upton* ISBN: *1-59462-222-1* **$13.95**
In the Cosmopolitan Magazine for May, 1910, and in the Contemporary Review (London) for April, 1910, I published an article dealing with my experiences in fasting. I have written a great many magazine articles, but never one which attracted so much attention... New Age/Self Help/Health Pages 164

Hebrew Astrology *by Sepharial* ISBN: *1-59462-308-2* **$13.45**
In these days of advanced thinking it is a matter of common observation that we have left many of the old landmarks behind and that we are now pressing forward to greater heights and to a wider horizon than that which represented the mind-content of our progenitors... Astrology Pages 144

Thought Vibration or The Law of Attraction in the Thought World ISBN: *1-59462-127-6* **$12.95**
by William Walker Atkinson Psychology/Religion Pages 144

Optimism *by Helen Keller* ISBN: *1-59462-108-X* **$15.95**
Helen Keller was blind, deaf, and mute since 19 months old, yet famously learned how to overcome these handicaps, communicate with the world, and spread her lectures promoting optimism. An inspiring read for everyone... Biographies/Inspirational Pages 84

Sara Crewe *by Frances Burnett* ISBN: *1-59462-360-0* **$9.45**
In the first place, Miss Minchin lived in London. Her home was a large, dull, tall one, in a large, dull square, where all the houses were alike, and all the sparrows were alike, and where all the door-knockers made the same heavy sound... Childrens/Classic Pages 88

The Autobiography of Benjamin Franklin *by Benjamin Franklin* ISBN: *1-59462-135-7* **$24.95**
The Autobiography of Benjamin Franklin has probably been more extensively read than any other American historical work, and no other book of its kind has had such ups and downs of fortune. Franklin lived for many years in England, where he was agent... Biographies/History Pages 332

Name	
Email	
Telephone	
Address	
City, State ZIP	

☐ Credit Card   ☐ Check / Money Order

Credit Card Number	
Expiration Date	
Signature	

Please Mail to: Book Jungle
                 PO Box 2226
                 Champaign, IL 61825
or Fax to: 630-214-0564

ORDERING INFORMATION
web: *www.bookjungle.com*
email: *sales@bookjungle.com*
fax: *630-214-0564*
mail: *Book Jungle PO Box 2226 Champaign, IL 61825*
or PayPal *to sales@bookjungle.com*

Please contact us for bulk discounts

DIRECT-ORDER TERMS

**20% Discount if You Order
Two or More Books**
Free Domestic Shipping!
Accepted: Master Card, Visa,
Discover, American Express

www.ingramcontent.com/pod-product-compliance
Lightning Source LLC
Chambersburg PA
CBHW081328040426
42453CB00013B/2339